SPIRIT BAPTISM AND THE 1888 MESSAGE OF

Righteousness by Faith

Dennis Smith

Printed in the USA

Unless otherwise noted all Scripture quotations are taken from the Holy Bible, King James Version.

Scripture quotations marked NIV are taken from the Holy Bible, New International Version. Copyright © 1973, 1978, 1984 International Bible Society. All rights reserved throughout the world. Used by permission of International Bible Society.

Cover designed by David Berthiaume
Text designed by Greg Solie • AltamontGraphics.com

ISBN: 978-0-9815736-3-2

Contents

Introduction 5

1 Ellen White and the 1888 Message 9

2 Jones and Waggoner's 1888 Message 15

3 The Baptism of the Holy Spirit 18

4 Christ Living in the Believer 27

5 Righteousness by Faith Alone 33

6 Complete Victory Over Temptation and Sin 39

7 Complete Victory Through Christ's Righteousness 44

8 Righteousness by Faith and the Third Angel's Message 63

9 The 1888 Message and the Last Generation 67

10 Preachers of Righteousness in Past Generations 74

11 Three Amazing Experiences 89

12 A Serious Warning 93

About the Author

A t the time of the writing of this book, Dennis Smith is serving as a pastor in the Southern New England Conference of Seventh-day Adventists. Dennis has served the church as an active layman and in pastoral and departmental positions for more than forty-one years.

Dennis received a Bachelor of Science degree in mechanical engineering from Colorado State University. While at Colorado State, he became a Seventh-day Adventist Christian. After working in engineering for a short time, he felt the call to full-time ministry. To fulfill that calling, Dennis attended Andrews University Theological Seminary and received a Masters of Divinity degree. Dennis has also studied in the area of public health from Loma Linda University.

In 1999, the Lord led Dennis and his wife Patty to begin studying the biblical teaching on the baptism of the Holy Spirit. As a result of their study, they were convicted to specifically pray for this biblical experience. Soon after they prayed for God to grant this infilling experience of the Spirit, a new spiritual life began to take hold of them both. Almost immediately Dennis felt led to begin writing about the things he was learning and experiencing. This book and the other books he has written are the result of that experience.

Introduction

I became a Seventh-day Adventist Christian when I was a young man finishing my studies in engineering at Colorado State University. One cannot become a Seventh-day Adventist without somewhere along the way hearing about the 1888 message of righteousness by faith.

I don't remember when I first heard about the wonderful yet sad time in our denomination's history when God brought to us the message of righteousness by faith. God had opened the understanding of two men, A. T. Jones and E. J. Waggoner, to this message. So they shared what they had learned about righteousness by faith at the 1888 General Conference Session in Minneapolis, Minnesota.

However, their message was not enthusiastically received by everyone. Many of our denominational leaders at the time were fearful of the message, feeling it would take us away from proclaiming the message our denomination was called to give—the three angels' messages. Therefore, it appears that the message did not have the impact on our denomination that God desired it to have.

Since becoming an Adventist more than 40 years ago, I hadn't given a lot of thought to the history of the 1888 message or studied deeply into what the message taught. I did come to realize it was about righteousness by faith and saw it as essentially teaching the justification aspect of righteousness by faith, which refers to Christ's righteousness being imputed to us or put to our account by our faith in Him. At first, I didn't see Jones and Waggoner's message relating to the subject of sanctification, only justification. With that understanding, I simply shifted to other studies.

In 1999, the Lord led me to look more closely at the biblical teaching on the baptism of the Holy Spirit. As a result of my studies, I specifically prayed to receive the Spirit's infilling. Soon thereafter, I began experiencing a revival in my personal walk with God and began seeing more power in ministry. Since that time, the Lord has led me to write several books on various aspects of the Holy Spirit. Each subsequent book expands on the experience into which the Lord will seek to lead Spirit-filled Christians, which is necessary for them to be ready for Christ's second coming.

The 1888 Message Brought to My Attention

A couple years ago while I was in the Philippines giving seminars on the Holy Spirit, a tall, blond-haired young man approached me just after I had preached the Sabbath morning message at Mountain View College. I had spoken on abiding in Christ and presented how we let Christ live out His life of obedience in our lives. Of course, no one knew the subject the Lord had given me for that morning's sermon topic. At that point, I had recently gained a better understanding of that aspect of righteousness by faith, and I had preached on this truth only a couple of times prior to that particular Sabbath morning.

The young man gave me a folder and said, "I think you will find this interesting." I looked at him, opened the folder, and read the title, "Easy," on what appeared to be an article. I repeated the title of the article "Easy" as I looked at the young man. He once again said, "I think you will find this interesting." Then he turned and walked away.

I didn't give much more thought to it until I was sitting in the airport waiting to fly back to Manila. I pulled out the folder and began reading the documents that it contained. Immediately, I saw that everything in it was about the 1888 message. The article titled "Easy" was by A. T. Jones on righteousness by faith. As I read, I realized that what he was saying was in essence what I had preached that previous Sabbath morning.

After I returned home from the Philippines, I received an e-mail and later a phone call from a retired pastor with whom I had worked many years before. He had read my books and commented that what I had written was quite similar to the 1888 message. Of all the men I know, he has done the most study into the messages Jones and Waggoner had given.

During this same time period, I also received a couple letters from individuals who had read my books, and they had commented that what I was presenting was the same as the 1888 message. I thought I knew in essence what the 1888 message was—justification by faith. So I didn't understand how what I had written about was similar to what Jones and Waggoner had taught since my focus was not especially on the justification aspect of righteousness by faith. The problem was, of course, my ignorance on Jones and Waggoner's teachings, which I now know included much on the sanctification aspect of Christ's righteousness.

Why I Wrote This Book

After these three experiences—the Mountain View College encounter, my retired pastor friend's comments, and the letters associating what I had written in my books with the 1888 message—I studied more closely into what Jones and Waggoner had taught. This book presents some of the things I discovered.

What happened in 1888, and the years that followed has been discussed, put in writing, studied in committees, and sometimes even created controversy. My goal in this book is not to give a detailed history of what happened or present everything Jones and Waggoner taught. The purpose of this book is to study what I consider the "core message" of their teaching—righteousness by faith. I will focus especially on the "sanctification" aspect of righteousness by faith, which I have discovered is often included in the term "justification" in Jones and Waggoner's writings as well at times when Ellen White refers to "justification."

As I have reflected on the significance Ellen White placed on Jones and Waggoner's message of righteous by faith and how it related to the finishing of God's work in this earth and preparing His people for Christ's return, I am compelled to write this book. The message of righteousness by faith taught by Jones and Waggoner is essential for God's people to understand and experience in order for the latter rain of the Holy Spirit to be poured out, for the last great message of warning to be given to the world in power (the loud cry), and for God's people to become just like Jesus in preparation for His coming (1 John 3:2).

Therefore, I will begin by presenting what Ellen White wrote about the message of righteousness by faith that the Lord brought to our denomination through A. T. Jones and E. J. Waggoner.

Chapter One

Ellen White and the 1888 Message

Ellen White understood that Christ's imputed righteousness (justification) and His imparted righteousness (sanctification) was absolutely essential for the believer to understand and experience.

> Clad in the armor of Christ's righteousness, the church is to enter upon her final conflict. "Fair as the moon, clear as the sun, and terrible as an army with banners," she is to go forth into all the world, conquering and to conquer. (*My Life Today*, 311)

> On Christ's coronation day He will not acknowledge as His any who bear spot or wrinkle or any such thing. But to His faithful ones He will give crowns of immortal glory. Those who would not that He should reign over them will see Him surrounded by the army of the redeemed, each of whom bears the sign, The Lord Our Righteousness. (*Maranatha: The Lord Is Coming*, 39)

It is only as God's people are "clad in Christ's righteousness" that they will be empowered to be victorious against Satan and his host. Only those people who are without "spot or wrinkle," without sin, will receive "crowns of immortal glory." How do they become without "spot or wrinkle?" The righteousness of Christ shines forth in and through them. They know by experience what it means to declare, "The Lord Our Righteousness."

Christ's Righteousness

"The Lord Our Righteousness" is the very message God gave to our denomination through Jones and Waggoner in 1888, and the years that followed. Following 1888, Ellen White herself wrote much about the importance of Christ's righteousness.

Christ's righteousness encompasses two important experiences in the believer's life. The first is called justification righteousness, which is imputed to the repentant sinner's life. Ellen White wrote:

> By faith he [the repentant sinner] can bring to God the merits of Christ, and the Lord places the obedience of his Son to the sinner's account. Christ's righteousness is accepted in place of man's failure, and God receives, pardons, justifies, the repentant, believing soul, treats him as though he were righteous, and loves him as he

loves his Son. This is how faith is accounted righteousness. (*The Review and Herald*, November 4, 1890)

In writing about Christ's righteousness becoming manifested in the believer's life, which is the sanctification aspect of righteousness by faith, Ellen White stated:

> The sanctification of the soul by the operation of the Holy Spirit is the implanting of Christ's nature in humanity. It is the grace of our Lord Jesus Christ revealed in character, and the grace of Christ brought into active exercise in good works. Thus the character is transformed more and more perfectly after the image of Christ in righteousness and true holiness. (*Selected Messages,* Book 3 [1894], 198)

Christ's very nature is implanted in the believer by the Holy Spirit. Every Spirit baptized believer has Christ living in him. If the believer asks and has faith in God's promise, Christ will live out His righteous life in the believer. The believer will then experience Christ's victory over temptation and sin because it is Christ living out His victory in his life. This is sanctification righteousness, which is imparted to the believer as he places his faith in Christ to "will and to do of his good pleasure" (Philippians 2:13).

> He who is trying to reach heaven by his own works in keeping the law is attempting an impossibility. Man cannot be saved without obedience, but his works should not be of himself; Christ should work in him to will and to do of His good pleasure. (*Review and Herald*, July 1, 1890)

Ellen White summarized justification and sanctification when she wrote:

> The righteousness by which we are justified is imputed; the righteousness by which we are sanctified is imparted. The first is our title to heaven, the second is our fitness for heaven. (*Review and Herald*, June 4, 1895)

The Heart of Jones and Waggoner's Message
These teachings on the justifying and sanctifying righteousness of Christ were at the very heart of Jones and Waggoner's messages of righteousness by faith. Ellen White emphatically supported their teaching on this subject.

The Lord in His great mercy sent a most precious message to His people through Elders [E. J.] Waggoner and [A. T.] Jones. This message was to bring more prominently before the world the uplifted Saviour, the sacrifice for the sins of the whole world. It presented justification through faith in the Surety; it invited the people to receive the righteousness of Christ, which is made manifest in obedience to all the commandments of God. (*Testimonies to Ministers and Gospel Workers*, [1895], 91-92)

Why Was the 1888 Message Needed?

Why was this message needed in 1888? Ellen White wrote:

Many had lost sight of Jesus. They needed to have their eyes directed to His divine person, His merits, and His changeless love for the human family. All power is given into His hands, that He may dispense rich gifts unto men, imparting the priceless gift of His own righteousness to the helpless human agent. (Ibid.)

Our denomination had become so doctrinally focused that Jesus had been lost in our experience and teaching. Our religion had become legalistic, which is the sure result of loosing sight of Jesus in one's life.

Leadership's Concern

Many of the leaders at the General Conference Session in Minneapolis reacted negatively to Jones and Waggoner's message believing that receiving it would cause our denomination to move away from giving the third angel's message, which God had called us to give to the world.

Ellen White addressed this concern when she wrote:

This is the message that God commanded to be given to the world. It is the third angel's message, which is to be proclaimed with a loud voice, and attended with the outpouring of His Spirit in a large measure. (Ibid.)

In another place she wrote:

God gave to His servants a testimony that presented the truth as it is in Jesus, which is the third angel's message in clear, distinct lines. (*Letter 57*, 1895)

In these statements she clearly associated the message of righteousness by faith with the third angel's message. She also stated that this was the message to be "attended with the outpouring of His Spirit in a large measure," which refers to the Holy Spirit's outpouring of the latter rain.

The Significance of the 1888 Message

She also declared that the message of righteousness by faith is the message to be proclaimed with a "loud voice" (loud cry) as the latter rain of the Holy Spirit is poured out. As this amazing message of Christ and His righteousness began to be proclaimed, Ellen White believed the loud cry of the third angel had begun. Of this she wrote:

> The time of test is just upon us, for the loud cry of the third angel has already begun in the revelation of the righteousness of Christ, the sin-pardoning Redeemer. This is the beginning of the light of the angel whose glory shall fill the whole earth. (*Review and Herald*, November 22, 1892)

Ellen White clearly associated the Holy Spirit with the message of righteousness by faith that Jones and Waggoner taught:

> The work of the Holy Spirit is immeasurably great. It is from this source that power and efficiency come to the worker for God; and the Holy Spirit is the comforter, as the personal presence of Christ to the soul. (*Review and Herald*, November 29, 1892)

Here she equated receiving the Holy Spirit with receiving the "personal presence of Christ into the soul." This happens through experiencing the daily baptism of the Holy Spirit, and it is only as Christ lives in the soul that His righteousness can be manifested in the life. Hence, the baptism of the Holy Spirit and the message of righteousness by faith are inseparably linked together.

Ellen White also linked receiving the baptism or infilling of the Holy Spirit with the earth being "lightened with the glory of God" (Revelation 18:1).

> When the earth is lightened with the glory of God, we shall see a work similar to that which was wrought when the disciples, filled with the Holy Spirit, proclaimed the power of a risen Saviour. (*Review and Herald*, November 29, 1892)

Just as the disciples were empowered to do Christ's work by receiving the baptism of the Holy Spirit on the day of Pentecost, so also God's last remnant people will need to be Spirit-filled in order to proclaim the third angel's message in power. The early rain, baptism of the Holy Spirit, must be received in order to benefit from the latter rain.

By bringing the message of righteousness by faith to His people, God was offering them the Holy Spirit in fullness.

The grace of the Holy Spirit has been offered you again and again. Light and power from on high have been shed abundantly in the midst of you. (*Testimonies to Ministers and Gospel Workers*, 97)

Glorious would have been the result if the Spirit had been received in fullness, and the message of righteousness by faith had been accepted by God's people following the 1888 message. The third angel's message would have been given in the power of the Spirit, Christ would have been perfectly reflected in the lives of His people, the loud cry would have gone forth, the latter rain of the Spirit would have fallen, and Christ would have come.

Christ is to be presented to the world as both a sin-pardoning Savior and a sin-delivering Savior. This is the full gospel message. It is when this full gospel of righteousness by faith is preached in all the world as a witness that Jesus will return. Preaching a gospel that presents only a sin-pardoning Savior is a partial gospel and will not fulfill Christ's promise and prophecy.

And this gospel of the kingdom shall be preached in all the world for a witness unto all nations; and then shall the end come. (Matthew 24:14)

This is why Ellen White wrote so emphatically about the necessity of the 1888 message of righteousness by faith being preached before Christ returns. It is the only message that will prepare God's people for that glorious event.

A Great Disappointment

That is how it would have been. However, sad to say, that is not what happened. Ellen White began realizing that the message was not being received as God intended. Expressing her great concern she wrote:

Neglect this great salvation, kept before you for years, despise this glorious offer of justification through the blood of Christ and sanctification through the cleansing power of the Holy Spirit, and there remaineth no more sacrifice for sins, but a certain fearful looking for of judgment and fiery indignation. (Ibid.)

It was a serious mistake for the denominational leadership to resist and even reject this God-sent message. Concerning this Ellen White wrote:

An unwillingness to yield up preconceived opinions, and to accept this truth, lay at the foundation of a large share of the opposition manifested at Minneapolis against the Lord's message given through Brethren Waggoner and Jones. By exciting that opposition Satan succeeded in shutting away from our people, in a great measure, the special power of the Holy Spirit that God longed to impart to them. The enemy prevented them from obtaining the efficiency which might have been theirs in carrying the truth to the world, as the apostles proclaimed it after the day of Pentecost. The light that is to lighten the whole earth with its glory was resisted, and by the action of our own brethren has been in a great degree kept away from the world. (*Letter 96*, 1896)

Here again she connected the Holy Spirit being imparted to God's people with the message of righteousness by faith. Both were rejected. Because of this, Ellen White wrote:

We may have to remain in this world because of insubordination many more years, as did the children of Israel. (*Letter 184*, 1901)

This prediction has certainly proved to be true. We have remained in this world more than 100 years since that statement was made.

God is calling His last generation into existence today. In order to be part of that generation who are ready to meet Jesus, we must understand and experience the baptism of the Holy Spirit and righteousness by faith.

Only those who are clothed in the garments of his righteousness will be able to endure the glory of his presence when he shall appear with "power and great glory." (*Review and Herald*, July 9, 1908)

Chapter Two

Jones and Waggoner's 1888 Message

Jones and Waggoner taught a number of biblical truths in 1888, and the years that followed. In this book I am focusing on what I consider to be the heart of their message—righteousness by faith in Christ. Righteousness by faith encompasses both Christ's justifying and sanctifying righteousness. I will focus primarily on the sanctification aspect of righteousness by faith that they taught.

The message of righteousness by faith comes through loud and clear in their writings. Following 1888, Ellen White also often wrote on the subject. God used the 1888 message to uplift Christ as never before to our denomination.

The core of their message contained several essential teachings. These teachings are listed below followed by quotes from Jones and Waggoner.

- In the flesh, Christ gained complete victory over temptation and sin. He lived a perfectly righteous life.

    } In Christ the battle has been fought, on every point, and the victory has been made complete. He was made flesh itself—the *same flesh and blood* as those whom he came to redeem. (*Lessons on Faith*, 129)

- When Jesus died on the cross, He died for our sins and broke the power of sin in the lives of all who believe in Him.

    } Thus every soul in this world can truly say, in perfect triumph of Christian faith, "I am crucified with Christ;" my old sinful human nature is crucified with him, that this body of sin might be destroyed, that henceforth I should not serve sin. Romans 6:6. (Ibid., 114)

- God calls every Christian to live a life of perfect obedience to His commandments.

    } Then it is plain that the first, the second, the sixth, the seventh, and the eighth verses of the sixth chapter of Romans all intend that we shall be kept from sinning. (Ibid., 144)

- It is absolutely impossible for any man, even the most committed Christian, to live an obedient, righteous life in his own strength by trying hard to obey God's commandments.

} Everybody has experienced it,—longing to do the good that he would, yet doing only the evil that he hated; having ever a will to do better, but how to perform it, finding not; delighting in the law of God after the inward man, yet finding in his members another law, warring against the law of his mind, and bringing him into captivity to the law of sin which is in his members; and at last, crying out, "O wretched man that I am! who shall deliver me from the body of this death?" Romans 7:14-24. (Ibid., 36-37)

• Through the Holy Spirit Christ lives in the believer. Because of this amazing union of Christ with the believer, Christ is present to manifest His victory in the life.

} Christ dwells in the hearts of all those who believe. ... Their lives are not from themselves, but it is the life of Christ manifest in their mortal flesh. See 2 Corinthians 4:11. This is what it is to live "a Christian life." (Ibid., 66)

• The only way for the Christian to live a victorious life over sin is to understand and experience righteousness by faith. As the believer places his faith in Christ who abides in him to live out His righteous life in and through him, he will have the victory.

} And there is the way to Christian perfection. It is the way of crucifixion, unto destruction of the body of sin, unto freedom from sinning, unto the service of righteousness, unto holiness, unto perfection in Jesus Christ by the Holy Ghost, unto everlasting life. (Ibid., 146)

• Absolute victory over all temptation and sin in the life is essential for all who want to be ready to meet Jesus when He returns.

} A. T. Jones quoted Revelation 10:7, which states that when the seventh angel begins to sound the "mystery of God" will be finished. Then he wrote: "But what is the mystery of God? 'Christ in you, the hope of glory. God ... manifest in the flesh.' Then in these days that mystery is to be finished in one hundred and forth-four thousand people. God's work in human flesh. God being manifested in human flesh, in you and me, is to be finished. His work upon you and me is to be finished. We are to be perfected in Jesus Christ. By the Spirit we are to come unto a perfect man, unto the measure of the stature of the fullness of Christ." (Ibid., 150)

This is a brief summary of Jones and Waggoner's core teachings, as I see them, on the sanctification aspect of righteousness by faith.[1]

Ellen White clearly articulated that reception of the message of righteousness by faith presented in 1888 would usher in the loud cry, the latter rain of the Holy Spirit, and hasten Christ's glorious return. With this exciting reality in mind, I pray that all who read this book will earnestly seek God for a clear understanding of righteousness by faith in Christ alone.

I personally believe Christ's second coming is imminent. So many events warn us of this fast-approaching event. Therefore, I also believe that God is rising up the last generation of Christians who He will use to lighten the earth with His glory (Revelation 18:1). All who participate in this last work of God must understand and experience righteousness by faith. That is why God is once again bringing this wonderful, hopeful, Christ-centered message to His people.

---

[1] In the following chapters I will present in greater detail these teachings with additional quotations from Jones and Waggoner.

Chapter Three

The Baptism of the Holy Spirit

U nderstanding and experiencing the baptism of the Holy Spirit is essential for the Christian to experience Christ's continual presence in our lives. It is only as Christ lives in us that His righteousness will be manifested. If we do not understand and experience the baptism of the Holy Spirit, we will not enjoy the fullness of Christ living in us, we will not have His righteousness manifested in us, or have the victories necessary to become just like Jesus and be ready for His second coming (1 John 3:2). Also, our service for Him will be less fruitful.[2]

Satan's Plan

Satan does not want us to understand or experience the baptism of the Holy Spirit. Ellen White was aware of Satan's devices to hinder the reception of this gift by God's people.

> Since the ministry of the Holy Spirit is of vital importance to the church of Christ, it is one of the devices of Satan, through the errors of extremists and fanatics, to cast contempt upon the work of the Spirit, and cause the people of God to neglect this source of strength which our Lord Himself has provided. (*The Great Controversy*, viii)

The baptism of the Holy Spirit simply describes a special infilling of the Holy Spirit into the life of the believer. This baptism is also called infilling and anointing, and has been available to Christians since the day of Pentecost 2,000 years ago. Peter associated the Pentecost outpouring of the Spirit with the "early rain" prophecy of Joel (Acts 2:16-21).

Jesus' Promise and Example

Jesus promised that the Father would give the Spirit to all who asked (Luke 11:13). Paul tells us that we receive this gift by faith (Galatians 3:14). The reception of this gift is so important that Paul commands us to "be filled with the Spirit" (Ephesians 5:18). This simply is not an option; it is a

---

2 I direct the reader to my book, *The Baptism of the Holy Spirit*, for a more in-depth study on the subject of Spirit baptism. If you have read that book this chapter will be a review for you. However, for the benefit of those who have not read that book I felt it necessary to include this chapter.

necessity if the believer is earnest about experiencing the full deliverance the gospel of Jesus Christ offers.

Jesus is our example in all things. In His life we see the baptism of the Holy Spirit as a special, separate event following His baptism. This event equipped Him for victory over Satan. It was also a special anointing for ministry (Luke 4:18-19).

Christ's experience is a divine model for every Christian. Christ was "begotten" of the Spirit (Luke 1:35). He was led by the Spirit in His childhood and early manhood (Luke 2:52). He received water baptism, which was followed by baptism in the Holy Spirit in answer to His prayer (Luke 3:21-22). From that point forward, He was filled with the Holy Spirit (Luke 4:1). After this experience of Spirit baptism (infilling or anointing), He was prepared to confront Satan and gain His great victories over this enemy (Luke 4:2-13). He went forward to minister in the power of the Spirit from that day onward (Luke 4:14; Acts 10:38).

The experience of every believer is to follow Christ's example. The Christian is first born of the Spirit and then baptized in water (John 3:5-8). However, water baptism is not enough; it is only the beginning. The believer must also be baptized or filled by the Holy Spirit (Luke 3:16, Acts 1:4-5). This Spirit baptism became available from the day of Pentecost onward. The infilling of the Spirit is necessary for the believer to have the power to live a victorious life and successfully witness for Christ (Acts 1:8).

Jesus said the believer would do the "works" He did and even "greater works" (John 14:12). When Jesus was on earth, He could only be at one place at one time. However, after He ascended to His Father, through the Holy Spirit He was able to be in many places throughout the earth by indwelling His followers (1 John 3:24; John 14:16-18). Hence, Jesus empowers the believer to do the same works He did by the Holy Spirit, and these works will be greater because they are more widespread and powerful.

The fulfillment of Jesus' promise was seen on the day of Pentecost and following. The gospel was preached, souls were won, unity and joy were seen in the believers, and the sick were healed (Acts 2:46-47; 5:15-16). This was the same type of ministry as Jesus' ministry.

Receiving the Baptism of the Spirit After Pentecost

Not every believer was present at Pentecost. A practical question might be, "How did believers receive the baptism of the Spirit after Pentecost?" The answer is found in the book of Acts. On a couple occasions the Spirit fell on a group while Peter spoke to them (Acts 10:44-46; 11:15-17). It also appears that God led the church to receive the baptism of the Spirit in a more orderly way by the laying on of hands (Acts 8:12-17; 19:1-6).

Note in Acts 8, the individuals of Samaria were led by the Spirit to accept Christ and be baptized. Yet, they had not received the baptism of the Holy Spirit. Peter and John went to them from Jerusalem for the specific purpose to lay hands on them and pray for the baptism of the Spirit to anoint them. This is a clear indication that water baptism and Spirit baptism are two separate experiences. The Spirit leads an individual to accept Christ and be baptized in water. The baptism of the Holy Spirit is a different work that must be sought separately when individuals become aware of its necessity. We see in Acts that Paul also received the baptism of the Spirit by the laying on of hands and prayer (Acts 9:17). In Paul's case, he received the baptism of the Holy Spirit before his water baptism. The one performing the prayer with laying on of hands should be a believer who has already received the baptism of the Holy Spirit.

When a member asks for prayer to receive the baptism of the Holy Spirit, the following prayer is an example that might be used with the laying on of hands on the head of the requester:

> Heavenly Father, we come into Your presence in the name of Your Son, Jesus Christ. When on earth, Jesus said, If we being evil know how to give good gifts to our children, how much more is our heavenly Father willing to give the Holy Spirit to them that ask Him (Matthew 7:11). And Your servant Paul said that we receive the gift of the Spirit by faith. So Father, we come before you seeking the baptism of the Holy Spirit for *(name)*. In the name of Jesus Christ I claim the promise of the baptism of the Holy Spirit for *(name)*. I pray that You will so infill *(name)* with the presence of Jesus that His character will be fully manifest through *(name)*. I pray that the fruit of the Spirit will be seen in *(name)* life and that *(name)* witness for Jesus will be attended as never before by the power of the Holy Spirit. Thank you, Father, for hearing our prayer. In Jesus' name. Amen.

A believer desiring the baptism of the Holy Spirit does not necessarily have to have someone pray for him or her with laying on of hands. When I first began sharing this teaching with our church, one of the members decided that very evening to seek the baptism of the Spirit. She earnestly prayed for God to fill her with His Spirit. She told me later that she felt the greatest peace that she ever experienced come over her.

God has not limited Himself to only one method of receiving the baptism of the Spirit. I do believe that the special ceremony of praying with laying on of hands is a wonderful way to seek the infilling of the Spirit.

It is always a special blessing to share in this sacred experience with a fellow believer.

God Calls Every Christian to Receive Spirit Baptism

Ellen White stated many years ago:

> What we need is the baptism of the Holy Spirit. Without this, we are no more fitted to go forth to the world than were the disciples after the crucifixion of their Lord. (*Review & Herald*, February 18, 1890)

> Impress upon all the necessity of the baptism of the Holy Spirit, the sanctification of the church, so that they will be living, growing, fruit-bearing trees of the Lord's planting. (*Testimonies for the Church*, Vol. 6, 86)

In reading Ellen White's statements on the baptism of the Holy Spirit, it is clear that she saw its importance and urged every believer to seek this indwelling. It was clear to her that the baptism of the Holy Spirit was essential for God's work to be finished in the lives of His people and in this earth. These statements also indicate that the Christian does not automatically receive the baptism of the Holy Spirit at conversion or water baptism. If that were the case, Ellen White would not tell Christians that this is an experience they need.

God sought to again draw our denomination's attention to this very important experience in the spring of 1928, when Elder LeRoy Froom was led to present this subject to delegates and workers at the quadrennial ministerial institutes held in conjunction with the union conference sessions. The book, *The Coming of the Comforter*, resulted from these presentations.

Referring to our neglect of understanding and receiving the baptism of the Holy Spirit, LeRoy Froom stated:

> I am persuaded that this is our colossal blunder. I confess it has been mine. We are not to "go" until we are endued. ... All true service begins at our personal Pentecost. (*The Coming of the Comforter*, 94)

Froom continued:

> For there is an experience beyond and above the initial step by which the Holy Spirit first reveals sin, and begets a new life in the soul, and that is to be filled with the Spirit. For the lack of this, one's testimony is feeble and the spiritual life but partial.

Alas, many today have gone as far as the baptism of repentance, but no farther. (Ibid. 142-143)

Froom's study led him to believe that the "baptism of repentance," which refers to water baptism was not enough. He concluded that the Holy Spirit's infilling is also necessary in order for the believer to be victorious through the time of trouble to Christ's coming.

It is a relationship into which we may or may not enter, though we are exhorted, yea divinely commanded to, in Ephesians 5; and in order to abide through the time when there will be no high priestly intercession, when mercy ceases and forgiveness for transgressions is ended, we must enter. (Ibid., 170)

Don't Let Satan Mislead

Because Satan fears this experience in the believer more than any other, he has spread much misinformation and confusion about what happens when a person receives the baptism of the Holy Spirit. He knows that the baptism of the Holy Spirit will break his power in the believer's life, and the resulting powerful witness for Jesus Christ will bring Satan's work to an end on planet earth. For this reason he has done everything he can to confuse this teaching and cause many sincere Christians to misunderstand it—even be suspicious of it.

There is nothing that Satan fears so much as that the people of God shall clear the way by removing every hindrance, so that the Lord can pour out His Spirit upon a languishing church and an impenitent congregation. When the way is prepared for the Spirit of God, the blessing will come. (*Review & Herald*, March 22, 1887)

Receiving the baptism of the Spirit does not necessarily involve a highly emotional experience. One may or may not feel something at the time of seeking the infilling of the Spirit. However, the Spirit will make Himself known to the one in whom He dwells. His presence will begin changing the believer's life from within his or her heart. A new power for victory and service will be manifested.

God desires to give His children this wonderful experience of Spirit baptism. However, in order to receive, we must ask in faith believing He will bestow it. Secondly, we must be willing to give ourselves completely to God.

The heart must be emptied of every defilement and cleansed for the indwelling of the Spirit. It was by the confession and forsaking of sin, by earnest prayer and consecration of themselves to God, that the early disciples prepared for the outpouring of the Holy Spirit on the day of Pentecost. (*Testimonies to Ministers and Gospel Workers*, 507)

Seek the Baptism Every Day

Another very important point is that we must renew this infilling every day. Paul said, "I die daily" (1 Corinthians 15:31). The dying to self and infilling of the Spirit is a daily experience. It is not a "once and for ever" experience. Paul tells us that the "inward man is renewed day by day" (2 Corinthians 4:16). We need the renewing of the Spirit every day of our lives. Also, Paul's command to "be filled with the Spirit" (Ephesians 5:18) is a continuous action verb in the Greek meaning we are to keep on being filled with the Spirit daily.

With the infilling of the Spirit the believer is led by the Spirit. Paul wrote of the importance of this being a daily experience when he stated:

For as many as are led by the Spirit of God, they are the sons of God. (Romans 8:14)

In this verse we find again that the verb form in the Greek is continuous action. Paul is saying, "As many as are continuing to be led daily by the Spirit of God." Thus, we must receive the Spirit everyday to be led by Him everyday.

Christ is our example in all things. Note what Ellen White wrote about the baptism of the Spirit in Christ's daily life.

Daily He received a fresh baptism of the Holy Spirit. In the early hours of the new day the Lord awakened Him from His slumbers, and His soul and His lips were anointed with grace, that He might impart to others. (*Christ Object Lessons*, 139)

Benefits of Receiving the Baptism

The baptism of the Holy Spirit gives power to our witness and brings forth the fruit of Christ's character in the life. Paul spoke of this when he wrote:

But we all, with open face beholding as in a glass the glory of the Lord, are changed into the same image from glory to glory, even as by the Spirit of the Lord. (2 Corinthians 3:18)

God's glory is His character (Exodus 33:18-19). Paul stated that the believer will be growing in Christ's character, "from glory to glory," (2 Corinthians 3:18) by the Spirit of the Lord that dwells in him.

The infilling of the Spirit of God will "make you perfect in every good work, to do His will, working in you that which is well pleasing in his sight, through Jesus Christ; to whom be glory for ever and ever" (Hebrews 13:21).

Ellen White reaffirmed the development of character the recipient of the Spirit's infilling receives when she wrote:

> When the Spirit of God takes possession of the heart, it transforms the life. Sinful thoughts are put away, evil deeds are renounced; love, humility, and peace take the place of anger, envy, and strife. Joy takes the place of sadness, and the countenance reflects the light of heaven. (*Desire of Ages*, 173)

We Can Grieve the Holy Spirit

There are things we can do that will grieve the Spirit (Ephesians 4:30). If we do not daily seek Him and cooperate in following where He leads us, His power will wane, and our Christian experience will weaken.

God doesn't force us to do anything. When we receive the baptism of the Spirit, He will have a greater impact in our lives. We will feel His promptings more strongly. The Spirit will daily put the desire in our hearts to obey God. He will call us to study God's Word and pray more. The Spirit will cause us to begin to love righteousness and to hate sin. However, we are always free to disregard His promptings. When we do this, we begin the process of "grieving" or "quenching" the Spirit. Paul gave very practical advice in many sections of Scripture on how to avoid doing this. Paul's practical counsel to the believer on living the Christian life are aimed at helping us to maintain the fullness of the Spirit in our lives. Two examples of such counsel are found in Ephesians 4:25-32 and 1 Thessalonians 5:14-19.

Paul knew that the Spirit of God dwelling in the believer would prompt him or her to do the things listed in these verses. If we refuse to yield to His prompting, we will be in danger of "grieving" and "quenching" the Spirit.

If you find that you have grieved the Spirit, don't be discouraged. Instead, ask God to forgive you (1 John 1:9), and He will. Then ask God to fill you anew with His Spirit, and He will (Luke 11:13). Ask Him in faith, and you will receive (Galatians 3:14).

David knew God was merciful. He had committed the sins of adultery and murder. He had walked away from the prompting of God's Spirit in his life when he committed these terrible acts. Yet, when he was convicted of his sin by the Spirit he turned to God in prayer (Psalm 51). Note especially these words:

> Hide thy face from my sins, and blot out all mine iniquities. Create in me a clean heart, O God; and renew a right spirit within me. Cast me not away from thy presence; and take not thy holy spirit from me. Restore unto me the joy of thy salvation; and uphold me with thy free spirit. (Psalm 51:9-12)

When we find that we have been slipping away from God, we must not let another moment pass without confessing our sin, accepting God's forgiveness, and claiming the promise of receiving the Holy Spirit to renew our lives as David did. Then we will once again be strengthened in the "inner" man to be victorious over Satan (Ephesians 3:16-19).

We Must Experience the Early Rain to Receive the Latter Rain of the Spirit

We are nearing the time for the "latter rain" to fall. If we do not experience the infilling of the Spirit, which is the "early rain" (Joel 2:23), we will not be prepared to receive and participate in the work of the latter rain. I believe God is moving among His people today and leading them into this wonderful experience.

If you have not received the baptism of the Holy Spirit, don't delay another day. His reception should be first and foremost in our lives. For this gift will bring all other gifts to us. The Spirit's infilling will change our lethargy to excitement, our weakness to strength, and our witness will be with a power not seen since the day of Pentecost.

A Necessity for Experiencing Christ's Righteousness

As I mentioned at the beginning of this chapter, for us to experience Christ's righteousness manifested in us we must daily experience the baptism of the Holy Spirit. Christ lives in us through the baptism of the Spirit (John 14:16-18, 1 John 3:24). This experience will lead us to become just like Jesus in our lives and service for Him. The Spirit-filled experience is not an option for those ready to meet Jesus when He returns. It is a necessity! Hence, it is my prayer that all who read this book will experience the Spirit's infilling every day. The baptism of the Holy Spirit must become a consistent part of our lives in order for us to have the faith to make it through the time of trouble, to experience full victory over temptation and sin, and to be ready for Christ's return.

No other way exists for us to relinquish our complacent, faithless, Laodicean condition and be prepared for the final crisis before Christ's second coming. Ellen White confirmed this with the words:

> Nothing but the baptism of the Holy Spirit can bring up the church to its right position, and prepare the people of God for the fast approaching conflict. (*Letter 15*, 1889)

I pray that you will take God's instruction seriously. If you are not daily claiming the promise of the baptism of the Holy Spirit do not let another day go by without seeking this marvelous blessing. For the Holy Spirit's infilling bestows all other blessings on you and will lead you into the marvelous experience with Christ.

Chapter Four

Christ Living in the Believer

When the believer receives the baptism of the Holy Spirit, he is actually receiving Christ more fully into his life. Moreover, Christ fully living in one's life is the only way to experience His righteousness in the life. Hence, the experiences of Spirit baptism, Christ living in the believer, and righteousness by faith are all closely linked together.

Jesus Lives in the Spirit-filled Believer

John tells us that the Christians who are living when Jesus comes will be "like" Him (1 John 3:2). How much like Jesus are we to become? The Greek word translated "like" means "just like" Him. How can this happen? Through the daily baptism of the Holy Spirit, Jesus will live out His life in us. Paul described this when he wrote:

> I am crucified with Christ: nevertheless I live; yet not I, but Christ liveth in me: and the life which I now live in the flesh I live by the faith of the Son of God, who loved me, and gave himself for me. (Galatians 2:20)

Through the infilling of the Holy Spirit, Christ will come and live in each of us. In the above text, Paul clearly stated that even though he was still alive, it was not really he that was doing the "living." No, it was Christ who was actually doing the "living" in him.

In several statements Paul taught this truth of Christ living in the believer.

> Examine yourselves, whether ye be in the faith; prove your own selves. Know ye not your own selves, how that Jesus Christ is in you, except ye be reprobates? (2 Corinthians 13:5)

> My little children, of whom I travail in birth again until Christ be formed in you. (Galatians 4:19)

In the above verse, Paul referred to the process of Christ being fully manifested (formed) in the believer.

> To whom God would make known what is the riches of the glory of this mystery among the Gentiles; which is Christ in you, the hope of glory: (Colossians 1:27)

Jesus living in us is our only hope of fully revealing His glory or character in our life.

Jesus' Promise

Jesus gave a wonderful promise to His disciples as He was about to leave them. He promised the coming of the Holy Spirit would result in Jesus dwelling in them.

> And I will pray the Father, and he shall give you another Comforter, that he may abide with you for ever; Even the Spirit of truth; whom the world cannot receive, because it seeth him not, neither knoweth him: but ye know him; for he dwelleth with you, and shall be in you. I will not leave you comfortless: I will come to you. (John 14:16-18)

Here, Jesus clearly stated that He would "come" to His disciples through the Holy Spirit. This took place on the day of Pentecost when the disciples received the baptism of the Holy Spirit. So it is through the Spirit's infilling that Christ lives in His followers.

The Benefits

Since Christ lives in the Spirit-filled believer, he or she will have the mind of Christ (1 Corinthians 2:16; Philippians 2:5). He or she will also have other attributes of Christ:

- His likes and dislikes
- His love of righteousness
- His hatred of sin
- His desire to obey the Father (Psalm 40:7-8)
- His passion for souls (Luke 19:10)

Paul told us that the wisdom, righteousness, and holiness of Christ was ours as Spirit-filled Christians (1 Corinthians 1:30)—every virtue and quality of Christ. We are to become more and more like Christ every day as we are changed into His "image from glory to glory, even as by the Spirit of the Lord" (2 Corinthians 3:18).

Christ living in the believer through the infilling of the Spirit causes the character of Christ to be fully developed in them. The Holy Spirit produces the "fruit of the Spirit" when He dwells within us (Galatians 5:22-23). This wonderful fruit of character will be manifested in the life more and more abundantly as the Spirit takes greater possession of the life. The Spirit will take such control of the believer that they will become like Jesus in every way (1 John 3:2). Ellen White very nicely described this in the following statement:

> All true obedience comes from the heart. It was heart work with Christ. And if we consent, He will so identify Himself with our thoughts and aims, so blend our hearts and minds into conformity to His will, that when obeying Him we shall be but carrying out our own impulses. The will, refined and sanctified, will find its highest delight in doing His service. When we know God, as it is our privilege to know Him, our life will be a life of continual obedience. Through an appreciation of the character of Christ, through communion with God, sin will become hateful to us. (*Desire of Ages*, 668)

The baptism of the Holy Spirit will bring about the fulfillment of Christ's promise that the believers will do the "works" He did and even greater works (John 14:12). Christ will do the same works today through the believer as He did when He walked this earth 2,000 years ago. This happens when the believer receives the baptism of the Holy Spirit and continues to walk in the Spirit. In fact, Jesus said the believers would do "greater works" because Jesus' works will be manifested through every believer that receives Him fully. In a very real sense every believer reflects Christ to the world. We become Christ's mouth, Christ's hands, Christ's feet, doing the very works He did: preaching, teaching, healing, casting out devils, etc.

Christ is our example in all things. Every word He spoke, and every work He did, was not really Him speaking and doing. He was simply an empty vessel in whom His Father dwelled through the Holy Spirit. Because of this Jesus said of Himself:

> Believest thou not that I am in the Father, and the Father in me? the words that I speak unto you I speak not of myself: but the Father that dwelleth in me, he doeth the works. (John 14:10)

Our experience is to be similar to that of Christ. Through the indwelling of the Holy Spirit, Jesus is to live in us, speak through us, and work through us. Our daily receiving the baptism of the Holy Spirit enables Christ to live out His righteous life of obedience in and through us. Our personal victory over temptation and sin is simply Christ's victory lived out in our lives. As a result, His righteousness will be seen in us as we choose to let Him manifest His righteous life in us and believe He will. This is righteousness by faith.

It is this full "manifestation of the sons of God" that the whole of creation awaits (Romans 8:19). When this occurs in its fullness the earth will then be lighted with God's character of glory, and the end will come (Revelation 18:1).

This full manifestation of Christ is also what Christ awaits.

> Christ is waiting with longing desire for the manifestation of Himself in His church. When the character of Christ shall be perfectly reproduced in His people, then He will come to claim them as His own. (*Christ's Object Lessons*, 69)

Notice in this statement by Ellen White that Christ is not waiting for you and me to simply become like Jesus by copying His lifestyle. No, Christ is waiting for the manifestation of "Himself" in us. Also, note that we are not to reproduce the character of Christ for Him. No, He is to reproduce His character in us for us.

Christ's Character and Works Made Manifest

The character Christ revealed, and the works He did, will be seen in the life of every believer that receives the baptism of the Holy Spirit and continues to walk in that baptism. That is why Jesus could positively state that specific signs would follow those that believe such as healing and casting out devils (Mark 16:15-18).

We see these words of Christ fulfilled from Pentecost onward. His character was manifested through all who received the infilling of the Spirit (Acts 2: 46-47). Thousands were won to Christ through the preaching of the gospel, and the sick were healed (Acts 5:15-16).

This wonderful work of Christ continued through the first few centuries of the Christian era. However, as darkness came upon the church through the many false teachings that were accepted and propagated, the church lost her power. The great era of apostasy brought with it great weakness in the body of Christ. The character of Christ became obscure, soul winning waned, and the healings all but ceased. A time of great spiritual famine griped Christendom.

Christians today are not exempt from these woeful influences. In fact, God in His message to Laodicea indicated that the last church of the Christian era, in which we now live, is failing to reflect Christ's character (Revelation 3:14-22). Unfortunately, however, she is unaware of her shortcomings. Laodicean Christians think that they have all they need. The church is "lukewarm," so she needs to be heated to become "on fire" for their Lord. Who has the needed fire? Jesus does. John the Baptist foretold that Christ would baptize with the Holy Spirit and fire

(Luke 3:16). The baptismal fire of the Holy Spirit is the only hope for the Laodicean church.

> I would that we had the baptism of the Holy Spirit, and this we must have before we can reveal perfection of life and character. I would that each member of the church would open the heart to Jesus, saying, 'Come, heavenly Guest, abide with me. (*Manuscript Releases*, Vol. 2, p. 26.)

Christ Wants into Our Lives

Christ is pictured as "knocking" at the door of the Laodiceans (Revelation 3:20). He longs to become a part of the lives of these professed believers, which is the only solution to their problem. The indwelling of Christ occurs only through the infilling of the Holy Spirit. The message of Christ to the Laodiceans is indeed a call to receive the baptism of the Holy Spirit, an experience that draws Christ fully into their lives.

When last-day Christians receive the baptism of the Holy Spirit and continue to daily walk in it, a great revival and reformation will be witnessed. Christ's character will be manifested in its perfection through His people by Christ Himself. God's last-day message will be proclaimed with a power not ever previously seen. Many signs will follow. Ellen White spoke of this time when she wrote:

> In visions of the night, representations passed before me of a great reformatory movement among God's people. The sick were healed, and other miracles were wrought. A spirit of intercession was seen, even as was manifested before the great day of Pentecost … Hearts were converted by the power of the Holy Spirit. (*Testimonies for the Church*, Vol. 9, 126)

The great focus of the prayers of God's people at that time will be to receive more of Jesus, more of the infilling of God's Spirit. The earnest desire of the heart will change. Instead of focusing on sin and lamenting their failures, they will be pleading "that I may know him" (Philippians 3:10). They have discovered the wonderful truth—to know Jesus is victory. This "knowing" comes through the infilling of the Holy Spirit. Victory comes by learning how to let Jesus live out His victory in the believer. Victory comes by fully experiencing righteousness by faith.

Christ will finish His work on this earth. We are all invited to participate in its glorious climax. However, the only way we will be able to work successfully with Christ in this work is to have Him working in and through us by the infilling of the Spirit. The only way we can have Christ live out His righteous life in us is by the infilling of the Spirit. That is why Paul so emphatically commanded us to "be filled with the Spirit" (Ephesians 5:18).

Chapter Five

Righteousness by Faith Alone

The great controversy has always been over Christ. We read in the book of Revelation about when the controversy first began in heaven (Revelation 12:7-10). Satan hates Christ and has always tried to replace Him (Isaiah 14:12-14).

The same controversy takes place in the lives of men and women today. Satan desires to reign on the throne of the heart. He wants mankind to follow his ways, not Christ's ways. In the area of Christian living, he wants to replace Christ's righteousness with man's efforts. He wants them to look to their own efforts for righteousness rather than Christ and His righteousness. He wants them to look to themselves for obedience rather than to Christ manifesting His obedience in and through them.

The Protestant Reformation's Theme

This issue was at the heart of the Protestant Reformation. The battle cry of the reformation was "sola fide," "by faith alone." This issue is at the heart of the gospel and the message of righteousness by faith.

The Bible is clear on the matter. Concerning the Christian's walk with God, Paul wrote:

> As ye have therefore received Christ Jesus the Lord, so walk ye in him. (Colossians 2:6)

The way we receive Jesus Christ as our Savior is by faith. We must believe that Jesus is the Son of God, died for our sins, forgives our sins, and gives us eternal life. We become Christians by faith in Christ. Works are not involved.

God does not require a lost sinner to begin doing good works before coming to Christ. The sinner does not have to "clean up" his life and try to make himself acceptable to God before receiving salvation. No, the sinner simply comes to Christ as he or she is and accepts Him by faith as his Savior.

Sanctifying Faith

Once one is born again and begins seeking to live the Christian life the new Christian naturally focuses on his or her own efforts to obey God's law. However, he or she soon discovers that this is impossible. Paul described this impossibility.

I find then a law, that, when I would do good, evil is present with me. For I delight in the law of God after the inward man: But I see another law in my members, warring against the law of my mind, and bringing me into captivity to the law of sin which is in my members. (Romans 7:21-23)

Paul had personally experienced the impossibility of obeying God's law through his own efforts. He was forced to cry out:

O wretched man that I am! who shall deliver me from the body of this death? (Romans 7:24)

He then gave the answer to his cry:

I thank God through Jesus Christ our Lord … (Romans 7:25)

A. T. Jones understood this struggle when he wrote:

Everybody has experienced it,—longing to do the good that he would, yet doing only the evil that he hated; having ever a will to do better, but how to perform it, finding not; delighting in the law of God after the inward man, yet finding in his members another law, warring against the law of his mind, and bringing him into captivity to the law of sin which is in his members; and at last crying out. "O wretched man that I am! who shall deliver me from the body of this death?" (*Lessons on Faith*, 36-37)

The apostle Paul had learned that faith in Christ was the only way to victoriously live the Christian life:

For what the law could not do, in that it was weak through the flesh, God sending his own Son in the likeness of sinful flesh, and for sin, condemned sin in the flesh: That the righteousness of the law might be fulfilled in us, who walk not after the flesh, but after the Spirit. (Romans 8:3-4)

Commenting on these scriptures, Jones wrote:

Thank the Lord, there is deliverance. It is found in Christ Jesus and in the Spirit of our God. Romans 7:25; 8:1,2. And the law of the Spirit of life in Christ Jesus having made you free from the law of sin and death, then 'walk in the Spirit, and ye shall not fulfill the lust of the flesh.' There is not only deliverance from the bondage of corruption: there is also the glorious liberty of the children of

God for every soul who receives the Spirit, and walks in the Spirit. (*Lessons on Faith*, 37)

In order to walk in the Spirit, we must daily experience the baptism of the Holy Spirit and choose to yield to the Spirit's promptings. Once we make the choice to yield to the Spirit's promptings we are to then look to Christ to live out His victory over the temptation in our lives.

Jones continued his description of the deliverance God offers the believer:

Walk in the Spirit, and ye shall not fulfill the lusts of the flesh.

See the list of the workings of the lust of the flesh: "Adultery, fornication, uncleanness, lasciviousness, idolatry, witchcraft, hatred, variance, emulations, wrath, strife, seditions, heresies, envyings, murders, drunkenness, revelings, and such like." None of these shall you fulfill, over all these things you have the victory, when you walk in the Spirit. It is the faithful word of God.

Is not that a most desirable prospect? Is not such a thing as that worth having? And when it is had for the asking and the taking, then is it not worth asking for and taking? (Ibid.)

E. J. Waggoner also described the all too common experience of many Christians.

There are too many who try to live the Christian life on the strength of the faith which they exercised when they realized their need of pardon for the sins of their past life. They know that God alone can pardon sins, and that he does this through Christ; but they imagine that having once been started they must run the race in their own strength. We know that many have this idea, first because we have heard some say so, and second, because there are multitudes of professed Christians who show the working of no greater power than their own. (Ibid., 2)

God and His Law Demand Righteousness

God and His law demand righteousness in one's life. However, because of the weakness of human flesh, attaining righteousness by keeping the law is impossible. Therefore, Jesus came in the flesh and fulfilled the righteousness requirements of the law; thus, He "condemned sin in the flesh." He was tempted in all points as we are in the flesh and was victorious over every temptation (Hebrews 4:15).

Because of Jesus' perfect and righteous obedience to God's law, when we have Jesus living in us we have His righteous obedience available to us. Therefore, Paul stated that "the righteousness of the law might be fulfilled in us." (Romans 8:4) You see, because of the "weakness" of our flesh we are unable to fulfill the righteous requirements of the law. However, if we have Jesus living in us through the baptism of the Holy Spirit, He will live out His righteous obedience "in us" if we place our "faith" in Him to do so. This is how we have Christ's righteousness manifested in our lives by faith.

No Righteousness Separate from Faith

Any righteousness that we seek to obtain by our own efforts is actually unrighteousness since it is impossible to attain to any righteousness apart from faith in Christ's righteousness. There is no righteousness separate from faith. That is why Paul wrote:

"For whatsoever is not of faith is sin. (Romans 14:23)

Concerning this truth, E. J. Waggoner wrote:

Without faith not an act can be performed that will meet the approval of God. Without faith the best deeds that a man can do will come infinitely short of the perfect righteousness of God, which is the only standard. Wherever real faith is found it is a good thing; but the best of faith in God to take away the load of the sins of the past will profit a person nothing unless it is carried right through in ever-increasing measure until the close of his probation. (*Lessons in Faith*, 2)

Waggoner continued:

We have heard many people tell how hard they found it to do right; their Christian life was most unsatisfactory to them, being marked only by failure, and they were tempted to give up in discouragement. No wonder they get discouraged: continual failure is enough to discourage anybody. The bravest soldier in the world would become faint-hearted if he had been defeated in every battle. Sometimes these persons will mournfully tell that they have lost confidence in themselves. Poor soul, if they would only lose confidence in themselves entirely, and would put their whole trust in the one who is mighty to save, they would have a different story to tell. They would then "joy in God through our Lord Jesus Christ." Says the apostle, "Rejoice in the Lord always; and again I say, Rejoice." Philippians 4:4. The man who doesn't rejoice in God, even though tempted and afflicted, is not fighting the good fight of faith. He is fighting the poor fight of self-confidence and defeat. (Ibid., 2-3)

The ONLY way to live a victorious Christian life is to look in faith to Christ (Hebrews 12:1-2). The ONLY way we can become righteous is by faith in Christ's righteousness. The ONLY way our obedience can be holy is by faith that Christ, through the Holy Spirit, will live His holy, righteous life within us. Jesus is the ONLY "way, truth, and life" (John 14:6). When we are tempted we can turn immediately to Christ to ask Him to manifest His victory over that temptation. Christ's righteous obedience will then be manifest in our lives. We will be experiencing righteousness by faith in our walk with the Lord. That is why Paul wrote:

For I am not ashamed of the gospel of Christ: for it is the power of God unto salvation to every one that believeth; to the Jew first, and also to the Greek. For therein is the righteousness of God revealed from faith to faith: as it is written, "The just shall live by faith." (Romans 1:16-17)

The true gospel of Christ is a gospel of "power." This power of Christ living in us gives us "salvation" through our "belief" or faith in Him. Thereby, the justified Christians live by "faith" in Christ alone for righteousness.

E. J. Waggoner wrote concerning this:

The gospel is God's remedy for sin; its work, therefore, must be to bring men into harmony with the law,—to cause the working of the righteous law to be manifested in their lives. But this is wholly a work of faith,—the righteousness of God is revealed from "faith to faith"—faith in the beginning, and faith to the end,—as it is written, "The just shall live by faith." (*Lessons on Faith*, 1)

Faith Overcomes the World

John recognized faith as the only means of overcoming the temptations of Satan.

For whatsoever is born of God overcometh the world: and this is the victory that overcometh the world, even our faith. (1 John 5:4)

You can see why Satan wants to blind God's people to the marvelous experience of righteousness by faith in Christ alone. First, he wants to replace Christ from that aspect of the Christian's life. Second, he doesn't want us to have victory over temptation and sin. He does not want God's law to be obeyed. For through experiencing righteousness by faith, we place

Christ at the very center of our walk with God, and our life will become one of obedience to God. Through our faith in Christ, obedience to God's law will be manifested in and through us by Christ. And that is true righteousness by faith.

Ellen White certainly understood the centrality of faith in the Christian's life. She wrote:

> The knowledge of what the Scripture means when urging upon us the necessity of cultivating faith, is more essential than any other knowledge that can be acquired. (*Review and Herald*, October 18, 1898)

She knew faith in Christ was the only way to victory. She knew that faith in Christ's righteousness was the only way to be righteous. She knew that faith in Christ was the only way to perfectly obey God's law. This is why she endorsed the 1888 message of righteousness by faith so strongly. She knew it was the only way to have Christ central in our lives and become the people who are ready to meet Christ when He returns in glory.

Chapter Six

Complete Victory Over Temptation and Sin

When you go on a trip, it is necessary that you know where you want to go. The same is true of our walk with God; we need to know where He wants to take us in our relationship with Him, and the victory we can have in Him over temptation and sin. In this chapter, we will consider where God wants to take us in relation to victory over sin in our lives. It is essential we understand this aspect of righteousness by faith. If we don't we will conclude that we simply have to continue with certain besetting sins in our lives until Jesus comes. The tragedy of that kind of thinking is that we will be lost if we are living when Jesus returns in glory.

Is It Possible?

Is a consistently obedient life really possible? Can we truly have victory over every temptation and sin in our lives? That is the kind of life God in the Bible calls us to live. The apostle Paul was very clear on God's will concerning complete victory:

Knowing this, that our old man is crucified with him, that the body of sin might be destroyed, that henceforth we should not serve sin. (Romans 6:6)

Likewise reckon ye also yourselves to be dead indeed unto sin, but alive unto God through Jesus Christ our Lord. Let not sin therefore reign in your mortal body, that ye should obey it in the lusts thereof. (Romans 6:11-12)

For sin shall not have dominion over you: for ye are not under the law, but under grace. (Romans 6:14)

John agreed with Paul's view of victory over sin:

Whosoever abideth in him sinneth not: whosoever sinneth hath not seen him, neither known him. (1 John 3:19)

Whosoever is born of God doth not commit sin; for his seed remaineth in him: and he cannot sin, because he is born of God. (1 John 3:9)

These verses clearly state that victory over temptation and sin is possible for the Christian. Ellen White also supported this view.

He who has not sufficient faith in Christ to believe that He can keep him from sinning, has not the faith that will give him an entrance into the kingdom of God. (*Review and Herald,* March 10, 1904)

Moral perfection is required of all. (*Christ's Object Lessons*, 330)

"The prince of this world cometh," said Jesus, "and hath nothing in Me." John 14:30. There was in Him nothing that responded to Satan's sophistry. He did not consent to sin. Not even by a thought did He yield to temptation. So it may be with us. (*Desire of Ages*, 123)

A. T. Jones' Teaching on Complete Victory

Jones and Waggoner also taught this. In a series of articles titled, "Christian Perfection," in the *Review and Herald*, July 18, 25; and Aug. 1, 1899, A. T. Jones gave a rather detailed exposition of Romans 6. The following are a few of his statements concerning the victory over temptation and sin the believer is to experience through Christ. They are taken from the book, *Lessons on Faith*, a compilation of writings by Jones and Waggoner. After discussing Romans 6:1, Jones wrote (page numbers appear in parenthesis):

Then doesn't he [God] intend that you and I shall be kept from sinning? And when we know that he intends it then we can confidently expect it. If we don't expect it, it will never be done. (141)

Referring to Romans 6:7, he stated:

Crucifixion, destruction, and then henceforth not serving sin, there, then, is the way to Christian perfection. (143)

He continued:

Then it is plain that the first, the second, the sixth, the seventh, and the eighth verses of the sixth chapter of Romans all intend that we shall be kept from sinning. (144)

After quoting Romans 6:13, he wrote:

The reign of grace lifts the soul above sin, holds it there, reigns against the power of sin, and *delivers the soul from sinning.* (Ibid.)

Thus from the first verse to the fourteenth of the sixth chapter of Romans, there is preached, over and over, deliverance from sin and from sinning. (Ibid.)

Then Jones summarized what he had presented on Romans 6.

It begins with freedom from sin; that is a great thing. Next upon that, freedom from sinning; and that is a great thing. Next upon that, servants to righteousness; and that is a great thing. Next upon that, unto holiness; and that is a great thing. And upon all, the end, everlasting life; and that is a great thing.

And there is the way to Christian perfection. It is the way of crucifixion, unto destruction of the body of sin, unto freedom from sinning, unto the service of righteousness, unto holiness, unto perfection in Jesus Christ by the Holy Ghost, unto everlasting life. (146)

Note also his emphasis on the necessity of the Holy Spirit in the victory Christ wants to manifest in our lives. The infilling, baptism of the Holy Spirit is absolutely necessary for complete victory.

E. J. Waggoner's Teaching on Complete Victory

Waggoner also taught that complete victory over temptation and sin is possible even now through Christ.

The overcoming is now; the victories to be gained are victories over the lusts of the flesh, the lust of the eyes, and the pride of life, victories over self and self indulgence. (*Lessons on Faith*, 3)

He acknowledged that many Christians do not have complete victory over sin and find the Christian life to be a great burden.

Some folks look with dread upon the thought of having to wage a continual warfare with self and worldly lusts. That is because they do not as yet know anything about the joy of victory; they have experienced only defeat. But it isn't so doleful a thing to battle constantly, when there is continual victory. (Ibid.)

Next, Waggoner asked the question, "Now how may we gain continual victories in our spiritual warfare?" Then he quoted John.

For whatsoever is born of God overcometh the world: and this is the victory that overcometh the world, even our faith. (1 John 5:4)

Waggoner was very clear that through the Holy Spirit complete victory is gained.

How the Spirit works in a man to subdue his passions, and to make him victorious over pride, envy, and selfishness, is known only to the Spirit; it is sufficient for us to know that it is done, and will be done in everyone who wants that work wrought in him, above all else, and who trusts God for the performance of it. (*Lessons on Faith*, 5)

It is only through daily experiencing the baptism of the Holy Spirit that the Spirit will be able to do this work of victory in us. Waggoner connected the work of the Spirit with Christ working in the believer.

Here is the secret of strength. It is Christ, the Son of God, the one to whom all power in Heaven and earth is given, who does the work. If he lives in the heart to do the work, is it boasting to say that continual victories may be gained? Yes, it is boasting; but it is boasting in the Lord, and that is allowable. (Ibid., 4)

Experiencing complete victory through Christ and through the Spirit are inseparably connected because Christ lives in the believer through the baptism of the Holy Spirit.

All Agree

The Bible, Ellen White, Jones, and Waggoner all agree that complete victory over temptation and sin is possible even now. The message of righteousness by faith presented in 1888 teaches us "how" we can have this complete victory through Christ living in us through the Spirit.

Complete victory is the experience we must all have if we are living when Jesus comes. That is why Satan has fought so fiercely to keep God's people from understanding the message of righteousness by faith. We need not fear Satan's plots against us. Jesus gained complete victory over our foe and offers that victory to us through our faith in His righteousness. Jesus began the work of salvation in our life, and He will bring us to complete victory as we place our faith in Him and His righteousness.

Being confident of this very thing, that he which hath begun a good work in you will perform it until the day of Jesus Christ: (Philippians 1:6)

Don't Be Discouraged

Don't be discouraged if you don't see this level of victory in your Christian life today. Learning the way of victory through Christ is a process.

As the disciple John wrote, God wants us to have the victory. However, if we fall we have Jesus Christ as our advocate with the Father. (1 John 2:1) Because of Christ's mediatory work as our High Priest we have forgiveness. (1 John 1:9)

Someday soon Jesus will complete His ministry as our High Priest (Daniel 12:1; Revelation 15:8). At that point we must have learned how to experience victory over all temptation and sin through righteousness by faith in Christ. Don't become fearful. Instead learn to daily, moment-by-moment trust Jesus to complete His work in you. (Philippians 1:6)

Chapter Seven

Complete Victory Through Christ's Righteousness[3]

I n Romans 7, Paul described the struggle every Christian has with temptation and sin in his life. Even though the power of the sinful nature was broken at the cross for the believer in Jesus Christ (Romans 6:6), that fact alone does not give victory over sin. The Bible is clear and untold defeats in every Christian's life confirm that we do not have the ability to overcome temptation and sin no matter how much effort we exert. Even if we ask God to add His power to our effort, we still fail.

A. T. Jones clearly described the impossibility of the Christian living an obedient life by putting forth effort to do so:

> Everybody has experienced it,—longing to do the good that he would, yet doing only the evil that he hated; having ever a will to do better, but how to perform it, finding not; delighting in the law of God after the inward man, yet finding in his members another law, warring against the law of his mind, and bringing him into captivity to the law of sin which is in his members; and at last crying out. "O wretched man that I am! who shall deliver me from the body of this death?" (*Lessons on Faith*, 36-37)

Until the Christian comes to understand and experience what it means to let Christ give him or her victory, he or she will not experience the consistently obedient life he desires. In this chapter, I will present how to let Christ live out His victorious life in you. When you come to understand and experience this truth, your Christian life will never again be the same. Instead of a life of sporadic obedience and broken promises to God, you will in time experience a life of victory through Christ over every temptation and sin Satan sends your way.

Just Like Jesus

We are fast approaching the second coming of Christ. The Christians who are living when Jesus returns will have gained the victory over every temptation and sin in their lives. John indicated this when he wrote:

---

3   This chapter is adapted from my book, *Spirit Baptism & Abiding in Christ*. In this chapter, I present the sanctification aspect of righteousness by faith, which is the "how" of victory over temptation and sin. It is at the heart of the message of righteousness by faith presented by Jones and Waggoner in 1888.

Beloved, now are we the sons of God, and it doth not yet appear what we shall be: but we know that, when he shall appear, we shall be like him: for we shall see him as he is. (1 John 3:4)

The Greek word translated "like" in this verse means just like Christ in character, nature, authority, etc. Christ was victorious over all temptation and sin, so those who are ready to meet Him when He returns will also be victorious over sin. In addition, the fact that they are living without Christ as their mediator indicates the level of victory they will have attained in Christ.

A. T. Jones presented this concept when he wrote of the completion of the mystery of God. He quoted Revelation 10:7, which states that in the days of the voice of the seventh angel, the mystery of God will be finished. Then he wrote:

> But what is the mystery of God? "Christ in you, the hope of glory." "God ... manifest in the flesh." Then in these days that mystery is to be finished in one hundred and forty-four thousand people. God's work in human flesh. God being manifested in human flesh, in you and me, is to be finished. His work upon you and me is to be finished. We are to be perfected in Jesus Christ. By the Spirit we are to come unto a perfect man, unto the measure of the stature of the fullness of Christ. (*Lessons on Faith,* 150)

Note again, this happens only by the Holy Spirit because it is through the baptism of the Holy Spirit that Christ lives in His people, and they grow into the fullness of Christ.

How Can It Happen in Your Life?

So what is the answer to how we can live a consistently victorious Christian life? The answer is letting Jesus live out His life in us. This truth is taught throughout the Bible. In the Old Testament we find references to it. David understood that victory came through God's presence with him.

> I have set the Lord always before me: because he is at my right hand, I shall not be moved. (Psalm 16:8)

> Thou wilt show me the path of life: in thy presence is fullness of joy; at thy right hand there are pleasures for evermore. (Psalm 16:11)

Isaiah understood the necessity of continual connection with God for victory and peace in one's life.

> Thou wilt keep him in perfect peace, whose mind is stayed on thee: because he trusteth in thee. (Isaiah 26:3)

The New Testament is very clear about the necessity of Christ living in us in order for us to have the victory over temptation and sin. Jesus used the imagery of the vine and branches to illustrate this truth.

> Abide in me, and I in you. As the branch cannot bear fruit of itself, except it abide in the vine; no more can ye, except ye abide in me. I am the vine, ye are the branches: He that abideth in me, and I in him, the same bringeth forth much fruit: for without me ye can do nothing. (John 15:4-5)

Paul taught this truth throughout his writings:

> Likewise reckon ye also yourselves to be dead indeed unto sin, but alive unto God through Jesus Christ our Lord. (Romans 6:11)

> We have the mind of Christ. (1 Corinthians 2:16)

Christ's mind was filled with pure, holy, virtuous thoughts. If we have asked Christ to live in us through the baptism of the Holy Spirit, if we believe He does, and if we believe He will manifest His love and His pure, holy, virtuous thoughts in our minds, He will do just that. It is a matter of faith—believing He will truly manifest Himself in our lives. Paul recognized this fact when he wrote:

> I am crucified with Christ: nevertheless I live; yet not I, but Christ liveth in me: and the life which I now live in the flesh I live by the faith of the Son of God, who loved me, and gave himself for me. (Galatians 2:20)

> That he would grant you according to the riches of his glory, to be strengthened with might by his Spirit in the inner man; That Christ may dwell in your hearts by faith. ... (Ephesians 3:16-17)

> I can do all things through Christ which strengtheneth me. (Philippians 4:13)

> To whom God would make known what is the riches of the glory of this mystery among the Gentiles: which is Christ in you, the hope of glory. (Colossians 1:27)

The Problem of Previous Definitions

I am sure that these verses are familiar to you. Most Christians know the words and phrases I am using and yet give them their own definitions of meaning.

Usually the personal application of these verses by the Christian is the belief that we must stay connected with God in order to have His power added to our efforts to obey. We often believe that Christ living in us means that He is there to strengthen us in our efforts to overcome the temptations and sins in our lives. However, that is not what these verses are saying.

The Bible is clear that our efforts are ineffective in overcoming temptation even when we have faith in God adding His power to our efforts. Paul described that ineffective method in Romans 7. We have all tried that method and failed again and again. So I challenge you to lay aside your definition of what it means to have Christ in you, and prayerfully ask "that the God of our Lord Jesus Christ, the Father of glory, may give unto you the spirit of wisdom and revelation in the knowledge of him: the eyes of your understanding being enlightened" (Ephesians 1:17-18).

He Was There All the Time

First, please realize that Jesus does literally abide in you. He said that He does, and we can believe Him. This happens as we daily receive the baptism of the Holy Spirit (John 14:16-18, 1 John 3:24). With Jesus living in us we have His mind (1 Corinthians 2:16), love, joy, peace, patience, gentleness, goodness, faith, meekness, temperance (Galatians 5:22-23), His likes and dislikes, His pure thoughts, His forgiveness; the list could be endless. Every virtue of Christ is in us through Christ abiding in us.

It is essential that we believe this fact. It is with this knowledge that we are to meet the temptations that come our way. However, even with this knowledge, the majority of Christians live their lives in the following way. They have accepted Christ by faith and believe they are forgiven. Then they think they need to work hard at becoming Christlike by putting forth efforts to obey Him. In their efforts to obey, they ask God to add His power to these efforts. As I have stated previously, all such efforts are doomed to failure.

What I am presenting is not becoming Christlike or always having Christ's help or power to resist temptation. What I am presenting is so much better than that. The truth is that Christ wants to literally live out His life in us; not simply add His power to our feeble efforts.

A. T. Jones wrote:

And remember that we are to be perfect with his character. His standard of character is to be ours. Yea, his character itself is to be ours. We are not to have one made like it: it itself is to be ours. And that alone is Christian perfection. (*Lessons on Faith*, 137)

How Does It Work?

How does this happen? Simply put, the steps are these:

- When you become aware of a temptation to sin, choose to turn your mind immediately away from it (Philippians 4:8).

- Believe that your sinful nature's attraction to the temptation is broken.

- Believe Jesus is in you.

- Ask Him to manifest His virtue in you in relation to the temptation. Be specific.

- Believe that He will manifest Himself in that manner.

- Rest in that belief, and don't fight the temptation. When we fight the temptation, we are actually focusing on it and trying to resist it in our own strength.

- Thank Him for the deliverance He has just given you.

Let's take the example of anger. Someone does something to make you angry. Perhaps they cut you off while driving or say something hurtful to you. The application of these steps would go as follows:

- As soon as you become aware of the temptation to become angry, choose to turn your mind away from what is making you feel anger.

- Believe that the "angry you" was crucified at the cross and that the power of your sinful nature's desire to become angry is broken.

- Believe Jesus is in you.

- Ask Jesus to manifest His "non-anger" or "peace" in and through you.

- Believe that He is doing just that at that very moment.

- Rest in that belief, and don't fight the temptation to become angry.

- Thank Him for the deliverance from anger He has just given you.

Another example is when you are tempted to think impure thoughts. Do the same thing with that temptation.

- As soon as you become aware of the temptation to think impure thoughts, choose to turn your mind away from what is making you think those impure thoughts.

- Believe that the "impure-thinking you" was crucified at the cross and that the power of your sinful nature's desire to think impure thoughts is broken.

- Believe Jesus is in you.

- Ask Jesus to manifest His "pure thoughts" in and through you.

- Believe that He is doing just that at that very moment.

- Rest in that belief and don't fight the temptation to think impure thoughts.

- Thank Him for the deliverance from the impure thoughts He has just given you

Every time you are tempted turn to Jesus. The temptation may be so strong that you may have to do this several times. That is OK. Through these experiences you are learning to abide in Christ's victory moment-by-moment.

Jones and Waggoner on the "How" of Victory

Jones and Waggoner presented this concept of victory over temptation and sin. Of this, E. J. Waggoner wrote:

> What wonderful possibilities there are for the Christian! To what heights of holiness he may attain! No matter how much Satan may war against him, assaulting him where the flesh is weakest, he may abide under the shadow of the Almighty, and be filled with the fullness of God's strength. The One stronger than Satan may dwell in his heart continually. (*Christ and His Righteousness*, 30-31)

Waggoner further described the victory the Christian can have through Christ.

> We have seen that we by nature are all servants of sin and Satan, and that as soon as we submit to Christ, we become loosed from Satan's power ... So then, as soon as we become free from the bondage of sin, we become the servants of Christ. Indeed, the very act of loosing us from the power of sin, in answer to our faith, proves God's acceptance of us as His servants. We become, indeed,

the bond-servants of Christ but he who is the Lord's servant is a free man, for we are called unto liberty (Galatians 5:13), and where the Spirit of the Lord is, there is liberty (2 Corinthians 3:17).

And now comes the conflict again. Satan is not disposed to give up his slave so readily. He comes, armed with the lash of fierce temptation, to drive us again to his service. We know by sad experience that he is more powerful than we are, and that unaided we cannot resist him. But we dread his power and cry for help. Then we call to mind that we are not Satan's servants any longer. We have submitted ourselves to God, and therefore He accepts us as His servants. So we can say with the Psalmist, "O Lord, truly I am Thy servant; I am Thy servant, and the son of Thine handmaid; Thou hast loosed my bonds." Psalm 116:16. But the fact that God has loosed the bonds that Satan had thrown around us—and he has done this if we believe that He has—is evidence that God will protect us, for He cares for His own, and we have the assurance that He that has begun a good work in us "will perform it until the day of Jesus Christ." Philippians 1:6. And in this confidence we are strong to resist.

Again, if we have yielded ourselves to be servants of God we are His servants, or, in other words, are instruments of righteousness in His hands. ... Our volition lies in choosing whether or not we will let Him work in us that which is good.

This idea of being instruments in the hands of God is a wonderful aid to the victory of faith when it is once fully grasped. For, notice, what an instrument will do depends entirely upon the person in whose hands it is. (Ibid., 105-106)

Notice Waggoner's continual emphasis on yielding to Christ for victory. This truth is simple but elusive. Waggoner emphasized this when he wrote that this truth "is a wonderful aid to the victory of faith when it is once fully grasped." Our problem is that we have not "fully grasped" it. Those ready to meet Jesus will have fully grasped and experienced it to such a degree that Jesus will be living out His life in them fully.

Waggoner went on to summarize the steps for victory over temptation and sin:

The whole secret of overcoming, then, lies in first wholly yielding to God, with a sincere desire to do His will; next, in knowing that in our yielding He accepts us as His servants; and then, in retaining that submission to Him, and leaving ourselves in His hands. Often victory can be gained only by repeating again and again, 'O Lord, truly I am Thy servant; I am Thy servant, and the son of Thine handmaid; Thou hast loosed my bonds.' This is simply an emphatic way of saying, "O Lord, I have yielded myself unto Thy hands as an instrument of righteousness; let Thy will be done, and not the dictates of the flesh.' But when we can realize the force of that scripture and feel indeed that we are servants of God, immediately will come the thought, 'Well, if I am indeed an instrument in the hands of God, He cannot use me to do evil with, nor can He permit me to do evil as long as I remain in His hands. He must keep me if I am kept from evil, because I cannot keep myself. But he wants to keep me from evil, for He has shown His desire, and also His power to fulfill His desire, in giving Himself for me. Therefore I shall be kept from this evil.' All these thoughts may pass through the mind instantly; and then with them must necessarily come a feeling of gladness that we shall be kept from the dreaded evil. That gladness naturally finds expression in thanksgiving to God, and while we are thanking God the enemy retires with his temptation, and the peace of God fills the heart. Then we find that the joy in believing far outweighs all the joy that comes from indulgence in sin. (Ibid.)

Here again we see that Waggoner emphasized our 100 percent dependence on God for the victory—not looking to our own strength. The key is in yielding ourselves into the hand of God and depending on Him for the victory. We are simply instruments in His hand.

A. T. Jones and E. J. Waggoner were in agreement concerning the victory the believer can have in Christ. In the September 1, 1896, *Review and Herald*, A. T. Jones wrote:

It can never be repeated too often, that under the reign of grace it is just as easy to do right, as under the reign of sin it is easy to do wrong. This must be so; for if there is no more power in grace than there is in sin, then there can be no salvation from sin. ... But grace is not simply more powerful than sin ... This, as good as it would be, is not all. ... There is much more power in grace than there is in sin. For "where sin abounded, grace did much more abound." ... Let no one ever attempt to serve God with anything but the present, living power of God, that makes him a new creature; with nothing but the much more abundant grace that condemns sin in the flesh, and reigns through righteousness unto eternal life by

Jesus Christ our Lord. Then the service of God will indeed be "in newness of life;" then it will be found that his yoke is indeed "easy" and his "burden light;" then his service will be found indeed to be with "joy unspeakable and full of glory."

Note the key points of Jones' statement:

- When grace reigns in us, it is easy to obey God. This has been the theme of this book. When we understand how to let Christ live out His life in us, there is no struggle with temptation. Why? We get the victory through letting Christ give us the victory, not by struggling with the temptation.

- Jones admonished us, "Let no one ever attempt to serve God with anything but the present, living power of God... "We receive the "present, living power of God" by daily receiving the baptism of the Holy Spirit. This is why it is essential that we understand and experience the Spirit's infilling. Without this, we have no power for victory or service.

- Righteousness will reign in us "by Jesus Christ our Lord." Jesus lives in us through the baptism of the Holy Spirit. His righteousness will be "imparted" to us, not just "imputed" to our account, as we learn how to let Him live out His life in us. Then we will not "let sin reign in our mortal body" or "obey it in the lusts thereof." (Romans 6:12)

The 1888 Message

The 1888 message was a message of righteousness by faith. It called God's people to look to Christ for pardon, complete justification, and full sanctified obedience to God's law through Christ's power. The believer was to have Christ's righteousness imputed to their account and declared righteous by God. Also, believers were to have Christ's righteousness imparted to their daily lives as they learned how to let Christ live out His life in them. The early-rain baptism of the Holy Spirit would do its work in preparation for the latter rain of the Spirit.

As you come to understand and experience this blessed truth of righteousness by faith, you will be allowing Jesus to live out His life in you every moment of every day. The victory is His. You are simply choosing to let Him manifest His virtues in and through you. That is your part—to choose, to give your will to God concerning a particular temptation. Yet, you are always free to not make that choice and focus on the temptation. When that happens, the sinful desire is conceived and will bring forth the sin (James 1:14-15).

Victory Over Bitterness

Perhaps someone has hurt you deeply. Sometimes in such situations we can experience what I call a "dark pleasure" by holding onto the anger and choosing not to forgive him or her. We feel that he or she doesn't deserve to be forgiven for the terrible thing he or she did to us. However, the Christian knows that God commands us to forgive those who have wronged us (Mark 11:25-26) and to love them (Matthew 5:44). It is for our own good that we forgive. Holding onto anger and not forgiving someone is like taking poison and waiting for the person we are angry at to die. Anger, bitterness, and lack of forgiveness will ultimately destroy us spiritually, emotionally, and physically.

Because of our sinful nature, the reality is that we are unable to forgive and love our enemies. We may do it intellectually, but our pride and selfishness will not allow us to forgive from the heart. In these cases, the same principle of deliverance must be followed. Jesus got the victory over the temptation not to forgive, and His victory can be ours. Jesus was also victorious over the temptation not to love those who abused Him. This victory can also be ours as well.

How can we allow Jesus to live out in our lives forgiveness and love toward someone who has hurt us deeply? Let's use the example of a person named Jim who has hurt you. You can simply say, "Lord, I am a sinner and cannot forgive Jim or love him. So I give up trying. I ask You to manifest Your forgiveness and love toward Jim through me. I trust You, and rest in the fact that You are doing this right now. Thank You Lord for the forgiveness and love you are manifesting in me at this very moment."

If you do this, you will experience Jesus' forgiveness and love in your heart. This will happen without any struggle to gain the victory. Remember, the victory was already gained by Christ's perfect life and death on the cross. You simply have to choose to allow Jesus to manifest His victory in and through you, and believe that He will. I can also say from experience that you will feel the compassion of Jesus for the person you are asking Him to forgive and love through you. You will feel within yourself the desire to pray for him or her and perhaps even with tears. In this manner, Jesus' character, love, and virtues become an integral part of your life.

Choose and believe—that is the Christian's part in obtaining the victory over every temptation and sin. Choosing means we give God our will on any given temptation. Where most Christians err is that they think giving God their will means they are to also exert their "will power" in order to obey. We are to give our will and let God provide the power by Christ living in us and manifesting His righteousness in and through us.

Thorns in the Flesh

This truth is presented when Paul describes his struggle with the "thorn" in his flesh.

> And lest I should be exalted above measure through the abundance of the revelations, there was given to me a thorn in the flesh, the messenger of Satan to buffet me, lest I should be exalted above measure. For this thing I besought the Lord thrice, that it might depart from me. And he said unto me, My grace is sufficient for thee: for my strength is made perfect in weakness. Most gladly therefore will I rather glory in my infirmities, that the power of Christ may rest upon me. Therefore I take pleasure in infirmities, in reproaches, in necessities, in persecutions, in distresses for Christ's sake: for when I am weak, then am I strong. (2 Corinthians 12:7-10)

Many things can be thorns in the flesh. Paul lists some of his; infirmities, reproaches, necessities, persecutions, distresses. Paul prayed for God to remove his thorn. God said no. Why? God's grace was all Paul needed in order to deal with the thorn.

God also gave a very important truth when He said, "My strength is made perfect in weakness." The weaker we know ourselves to be and the sooner we stop trying to exert our puny strength to overcome a thorny temptation in our lives, the sooner we will begin experiencing God's mighty power in our lives. Our own exertion of effort to overcome a temptation actually gets in the way of God's power to deliver. You see, when we do that we are looking to our strength and ability to overcome even though we think we are also depending on God to "help" us. God wants to do much more than "help" us. *He is the victory. Christ is our deliverance from temptation.* When we back away from such efforts and get ourselves out of the way, then Christ can begin manifesting Himself in and through us. You have probably heard the saying, "Let go, and let God." This is what that saying means.

The prophet Isaiah understood the importance of recognizing our utter weakness in order to experience God's power.

> He giveth power to the faint; and to them that have no might he increaseth strength. (Isaiah 40:29)

E. J. Waggoner described the futility of the sinners' efforts to obey God.

> We have heard many people tell how hard they found it to do right; their Christian life was most unsatisfactory to them, being marked only by failure, and they were tempted to give up in discouragement. No wonder they get discouraged: continual failure

is enough to discourage anybody. The bravest soldier in the world would become faint-hearted if he had been defeated in every battle. Sometimes these persons will mournfully tell that they have lost confidence in themselves. Poor soul, if they would only lose confidence in themselves entirely, and would put their whole trust in the one who is mighty to save, they would have a different story to tell. They would then 'joy in God through our Lord Jesus Christ.' Says the apostle, 'Rejoice in the Lord always; and again I say, Rejoice.' Philippians 4:4. The man who doesn't rejoice in God, even though tempted and afflicted, is not fighting the good fight of faith. He is fighting the poor fight of self-confidence and defeat. (*Lessons on Faith*, 2-3)

How clearly Waggoner stated the truth of those who struggle for victory, "Sometimes these persons will mournfully tell that they have lost confidence in themselves. Poor soul, if they would only lose confidence in themselves entirely, and would put their whole trust in the one who is mighty to save, they would have a different story to tell." Yes, lose confidence in yourself! Yes, put your whole trust in Jesus!

This is why the Lord will leave some thorns of temptation in your life. I am sure you have prayed for God to remove these thorns of besetting sins. They have brought such discouragement and defeat in your life. However, God leaves them because He wants you to learn the lesson that His strength is made perfect in your weakness. When you begin experiencing Christ's deliverance in you, then you along with Paul will declare, "Most gladly therefore will I rather glory in my infirmities, that the power of Christ may rest upon me. Therefore I take pleasure in infirmities, in reproaches, in necessities, in persecutions, in distresses for Christ's sake: for when I am weak, then am I strong" (2 Corinthians 12:9-10)

Thank You for the Thorns!

You will come to the point that you actually thank God for the thorns in your life. Why? It is because of them that you experience the amazing delivering power of Christ. Because of them, Christ has become even more precious to you. You have found Him giving you ever-present victories over your temptations, and praises of Him fill your heart.

You also rejoice in the thorns because they are opportunities for God's glory to shine forth through you as Christ manifests His righteous life in and through you. They are opportunities for you to become more and more like Christ in those areas of your life as He manifests Himself more and more in your life.

James addressed this when he wrote:

My brethren, count it all joy when ye fall into diverse temptations; knowing this, that the trying of your faith worketh patience [endurance]. But let patience have her perfect work, that ye may be perfect and entire, wanting nothing. (James 1:2-4)

You will then experience what Paul describes "as sorrowful, yet always rejoicing" (2 Corinthians 6:10). Even in the midst of the most difficult circumstances you will be able to rejoice because Jesus will manifest Himself in you. Your faith in Christ develops an endurance that will lead to Christ manifesting Himself in you fully.

Christ Manifest in the Flesh

You are the temple of God, and it is His desire to "dwell in you and walk in you" (2 Corinthians 6:16). Jesus wants to live out His life in you. He wants to manifest all His righteous virtues, character, and obedience in and through you. If you choose to turn from your temptations and trust Him to manifest Himself, He will. In fact, Christ will become so much a part of your mind, body, and soul that He, through you, will be once again manifest in the flesh—in your flesh. Ellen White described this experience.

All true obedience comes from the heart. It was heart work with Christ. And if we consent, He will so identify Himself with our thoughts and aims, so blend our hearts and minds into conformity to His will, that *when obeying Him we shall be but carrying out our own impulses*. The will, refined and sanctified, will find its highest delight in doing His service. When we know God, as it is our privilege to know Him, *our lives will be a life of continual obedience*. Through an appreciation of the character of Christ, through communion with God, sin will become hateful to us. (*Desire of Ages*, 668, emphasis added)

These words describe those who are ready to meet Jesus when He returns. When obeying Him, they will be simply carrying out their own impulses because Christ is fully manifest in and through them. Their life will be one of continual obedience because they allow Christ to live out His life in them continually. This is the high and holy calling God is giving to you today.

This is not a call to try harder or put forth more effort to obey. It is a call to be filled with His Spirit, choose to obey Him in all things, and let Christ manifest His righteousness in and through you. When you say yes to His call and learn how to let Christ live out His life in you, your Christian life will no longer be a burden. As recorded in the gospel of Matthew, Christ offered:

> Come unto me, all ye that labor and are heavy laden, and I will give you rest. Take my yoke upon you, and learn of me; for I am meek and lowly in heart: and ye shall find rest unto your soul. For my yoke is easy, and my burden is light. (Matthew 11:28-30)

Referring to those who seek to serve God, Ellen White wrote:

> The inexhaustible supplies of heaven are at their command. Christ gives them the breath of His own Spirit, the life of His own life. The Holy Spirit puts forth its highest energies to work in heart and mind. (*Testimonies for the Church*, Vol. 6, 306)

Here we are told that the believer has Christ's very life through the Holy Spirit's presence, and that the Spirit brings about marvelous changes in the heart and mind of the believer.

E. J. Waggoner clearly taught the same thing:

> This endless, spotless life Christ gives to all who believe on Him … Christ dwells in the hearts of all those who believe on Him …

> Christ, the light of the world, dwelling in the hearts of his followers, constitutes them the light of the world. Their light comes not from themselves, but from Christ, who dwells in them. Their lives are not from themselves; but it is the life of Christ manifest in their mortal flesh. See 2 Corinthians 4:11. This is what it is to live "a Christian life." (*Lessons on Faith*, 66)

In another place, Ellen White explained the amazing miracle of transformation further.

> When His words of instruction have been received, and have taken possession of us, Jesus is to us an abiding presence, controlling our thoughts, and ideas and actions … It is no more we that live, but Christ that liveth in us, and he is the hope of glory. Self is dead, but Christ is a living Saviour. (*Testimonies to Ministers and Gospel Workers*, 389)

Ellen White was very clear on the matter. She clearly stated that it is Jesus' abiding presence that controls our thoughts, ideas, and actions. If we choose to believe that He will do this and believe our sinful nature's power over us is dead, then Christ will most definitely live out His life in us. It is just that simple!

As this process continues in believers' lives who, for example, previously had impure thoughts whenever he saw a woman, especially if she was scantily dressed, will now have only pure thoughts when he sees such a woman. In situations where anger would have arisen in the past, there is no anger now. Where certain unhealthy foods would have triggered a craving, now there is no craving. These are examples as to how much Christ will be manifested in those who choose to let Him do so. The power of the sinful nature will be totally subdued, and Christ's sinless nature will be totally dominant in the life.

However, it is important to remember this is a process. Such dramatic changes don't usually happen instantly. We must daily grow in the experience of letting Christ live out His life in us. A. T. Jones wrote of this in the following way:

> This [growing up into Christ in all things] is to be accomplished in you and me by growth; but there can be no growth where there is no life. This is growth in the knowledge of God, growth in the wisdom of God, growth in the character of God, growth in God; therefore, it can be only by the life of God. (*Lessons on Faith*, 148)

Be Enlightened

In short, whatever attitudes or behavior the Lord asks us to exhibit, He will manifest in and through us if we choose to let Him and believe He will. This requires us to be aware of the attitudes and behaviors God wants us to exhibit. We find this instruction in the Word of God.

God's standard is high, so high that it is impossible for us to meet it. This standard will be met only as Christ lives out this standard through us. Paul actually points this out in his letter to the Romans.

> For what the law was powerless to do in that it was weakened by the sinful nature, God did by sending his own Son in the likeness of sinful man to be a sin offering. And so he condemned sin in sinful man, in order that the righteous requirements of the law might be fully met in us, who do not live according to the sinful nature but according to the Spirit. (Romans 8:3-4; NIV)

In these verses, Paul shared with us that it is impossible for sinful mankind to fulfill the righteous requirements of God's law. However, because Christ came in the flesh, obeyed the law perfectly, and fulfilled all the righteous requirements of the law, He condemned sin breaking its power. Therefore, through Christ the "righteous requirements of the law" can be "fully met in us" who do not yield to our sinful natures, but allow the Spirit to manifest obedience in us.

New-covenant Promise

This chapter presents how God fulfills the new-covenant promise. In the new covenant, God says He will write His law on our hearts and in our minds (Hebrews 8:8-10). Our part is to choose to allow Him to do it. God foretold through the prophet Ezekiel that He would do this.

> Then I will sprinkle clean water upon you, and ye shall be clean: from all your filthiness and from all your idols, will I cleanse you. A new heart also will I give you, and a new spirit will I put within you: and I will take away the stony heart out of your flesh, and I will give you an heart of flesh. And I will put my spirit within you, and cause you to walk in my statutes, and ye shall keep my judgments, and do them. (Ezekiel 36:25-27)

The New Testament confirms this promise in texts such as the following:

> Being confident of this very thing, that he which hath begun a good work in you, will perform it until the day of Jesus Christ. (Philippians 1:6)

Note that it is God who "performs" this work. Paul presents this same truth in his first letter to the Thessalonians.

> And the very God of peace sanctify you wholly; and I pray God your whole spirit and soul and body be preserved blameless unto the coming of our Lord Jesus Christ. Faithful is he that calleth you, who also will do it. (1 Thessalonians 5:23-24)

Again, Paul was clear; God does the sanctifying. Our part is to choose to allow Him to perform that work within our spirit, soul, and body.

Lighten Up

All Christians who are not experiencing deliverance from temptation through Christ, but are trying to do it through their own efforts by asking God to add His power to their efforts are not experiencing the "light burden" Jesus referenced in Matthew 11:28-29. Instead, their lives are weighed down with frustration, bewilderment, and feelings of defeat. Jesus calls us to come to Him with this burden. If you learn how to do that, you will find "rest," and your walk with the Lord will become much "easier" and "lighter" because Jesus is giving you His victory, and you are resting in Him for the victory.

Before I came to personally understand and experience the reality of abiding in Christ and allowing Him to manifest Himself in and through me, I did not understand these words of Christ. For me the Christian life was a burden and obedience was not easy. Once I came to understand and experience Christ's abiding presence, only then did I find His words to be true—"My yoke is easy, and my burden is light." He offers the same abiding experience to all who believe in Him.

Stay in Touch

This kind of victory in Christ requires us to be in moment-by-moment communion with Him. Remember that David wrote, "I have set the LORD always before me: because he is at my right hand, I shall not be moved" (Psalm 16:8). David knew the necessity of the Lord being "always before him." We must not let our communion with Jesus be broken.

We can also see that the victory Jesus offers us requires a moment-by-moment surrender to Him. Whenever a temptation comes we must surrender it to Him no matter how much we have enjoyed yielding to it in the past. Complete 100 percent surrender is the only way to complete 100 percent victory.

Ellen White wrote of the necessity of moment-by-moment communion and surrender with the words:

> We may leave off many bad habits, for the time we may part company with Satan; but without a vital connection with God, through the surrender of ourselves to him moment-by-moment we shall be overcome. Without a personal acquaintance with Christ, and a continual communion, we are at the mercy of the enemy, and shall do his bidding in the end. (*Desire of Ages*, 324)

Daily receiving the baptism of the Holy Spirit is also essential for our communion with Christ to remain unbroken. Ellen White confirmed this when she wrote:

> We must have a living connection with God. We must be clothed with power from on high by the baptism of the Holy Spirit, that we may reach a higher standard; for there is help for us in no other way. (*Review and Herald,* April 5, 1892)

We are clearly told that the baptism of the Holy Spirit is what gives us a "living connection" with God. We are also told that the Spirit's infilling is *absolutely necessary* for this to happen. As she stated, "There is help for us in no other way."

Christ—Our Only Hope

The message of righteousness by faith was a message of hope, a message of victory, a message that lifted up Jesus. It taught Jesus as our only hope of victory and being ready for His glorious return.

I personally believe the Lord is reissuing this message to His people. May we not repeat the experience of those who have gone before us. May we earnestly seek the Lord for a clear understanding of the message, asking Him to lead us into the fullness of Christ living in us and manifesting His righteousness.

The generation to which that message was given failed to receive it. It appears that several generations following them also failed to receive it. I challenge today's generation not to follow their sad example. May we take seriously God's call to be filled with His Spirit and experience the full manifestation of Christ in our lives and service for Him. This is why our Lord is waiting for us.

> Christ is waiting with longing desire for the manifestation of Himself in His church. When the character of Christ shall be perfectly reproduced in His people, then He will come to claim them as His own. (*Christ's Object Lessons*, 69)

Christ is waiting for the manifestation of Himself in His people. He is not waiting for them to simply become "like" Him. No, He is waiting for He Himself to be manifested and seen. He is also waiting for His character to be "perfectly reproduced" in His people. He is not waiting for us to reproduce His character within ourselves for Him. No, He is waiting for us to allow Him to reproduce His character in us by living out His righteousness in us. These things can only happen as we understand and experience the message of righteousness by faith presented in 1888.

Waggoner described this experience as follows:

> Here is the secret of strength. It is Christ, the Son of God, the one to whom all power in Heaven and earth is given, who does the work. If he lives in the heart to do the work, is it boasting to say that continual victories may be gained? Yes, it is boasting; but it is boasting in the Lord, and that is allowable. (*Lesson on Faith*, 4)

Once you discover this amazing truth of experiencing Christ's righteousness your life will never be the same again. Your life will be filled with joy and peace. You will see victories previously thought impossible to attain. Jesus will be everything to you. You will know from experience what Paul meant when he wrote, "Christ in you, the hope of glory" (Colossians 1:27).

Chapter Eight

Righteousness by Faith and the Third Angel's Message

When the message of righteousness by faith was presented at the 1888 General Conference Session by Jones and Waggoner, many in leadership believed its acceptance and emphasis would lead our denomination away from fulfilling the mission God had given us and preaching the third angel's message. The Seventh-day Adventist Church had been raised up by the Lord to give the last-warning message to the world. We were called to uplift God's Ten Commandments, including the seventh-day Sabbath of the fourth commandment. This commission involved warning the world of Satan's plan to lead men and women away from God's commandments and to accept his counterfeit day of worship (Revelation 13).

Responses to the Message

The denominational leadership took this mission very seriously. Many had been in the work for many years and thought they knew well what this mission involved. When Jones and Waggoner presented their messages on righteousness by faith, the denominational leadership didn't see where this teaching fit into the mission the Lord had given us. They even deemed it to be dangerous.

A well-known denominational leader and General Conference president, Arthur G. Daniels, was asked by the Ministerial Association Advisory Council in 1924 to "arrange for a compilation of the writings of Mrs. E. G. White on the subject of justification by faith." (*Christ Our Righteousness*, 5) The result of Daniel's work was the book, *Christ Our Righteousness*. In that book, he wrote what he believed took place when Jones and Waggoner presented the message of righteousness by faith. He divided the response into three classes.

Class 1—Those who saw great light in it and gladly accepted it; who believed it to be a most essential phase of the gospel, and felt that it should be given great emphasis in all efforts to save the lost. To this class the message appeared to be the real secret of a victorious life in the conflict with sin, and that the great truth of being made righteous by faith in the Son of God was the most pressing need of the remnant church in preparing for translation at the second advent.

Class 2—There were some, however, who felt uncertain about the "new teaching," as they termed it. They seemed unable to grasp it. They could not reach a conclusion. As a result, their minds were thrown into a state of perplexity and confusion. They neither accepted nor rejected the message at the time.

Class 3—But there were others who were decidedly opposed to the presentation of the message. They claimed that the truth of righteousness by faith had been recognized by our people from the very first, and this was true theoretically. For this reason they saw no occasion for placing such great stress and emphasis upon the subject as was being done by its advocates. Furthermore, they feared that the emphasis placed upon this theme of righteousness by faith would cast a shadow upon the doctrines that had been given such prominence from the beginning of our denominational history; and since they looked upon the preaching of those distinctive doctrines as the secret of the power and growth of the movement, they were fearful that if these doctrines were overshadowed by any teaching or message whatsoever, our cause would lose its distinctive character and force. Because of these fears, they felt in duty bound to safeguard both cause and people by decided opposition. (*Christ Our Righteousness*, 41-42)

Ellen White's View

Ellen White supported the views of the first class mentioned in Daniel's representation of the three classes. Moreover, she was very strong in her counsel to those who rejected it:

Some have turned from the message of the righteousness of Christ to criticize the men ... The third angel's message will not be comprehended, the light which will lighten the earth with its glory will be called a false light, by those who refuse to walk in its advancing glory. The work that might have been done, will be left undone by the rejecters of truth, because of their unbelief. We entreat of you who oppose the light of truth, to stand out of the way of God's people. Let Heaven-sent light shine forth upon them in clear and steady rays. God holds you to whom this light has come, responsible for the use you make of it. Those who will not hear will be held responsible; for the truth has been brought within their reach, but they despised their opportunities and privileges. (*Review and Herald*, May 27, 1890)

She had been a part of the advent movement since its beginning and saw no danger in this message taking the people away from the mission the Lord had given to this church; to preach the third angel's message. She addressed this concern in the following statement.

> Several have written to me, inquiring if the message of justification by faith is the third angel's message, and I have answered, "It is the third angel's message in verity." (*Review and Herald*, April 1, 1890)

How Are Righteousness by Faith and the Third Angel's Message Related?

Some may still ask the same question today, "What does the message of righteousness by faith have to do with the third angel's message?"

I would begin by asking, "What is the purpose of the third angel's message?" The third angel's message calls men and women to obedience of God's commandments, including the fourth commandment admonishing mankind to keep holy the seventh-day Sabbath. The message includes a warning to all who turn from God and receive the "mark of the beast," which is Satan's counterfeit day of worship. Those who receive the mark of the beast will experience the seven last plagues and be lost. (Revelation 14:9-10)

The next question I would ask is, "What is the purpose of the message of righteousness by faith in Christ?" The answer is: the message of righteousness by faith leads men and women to obedience of God's commandments as they in faith allow Christ to live out His life of righteous obedience to God's law. Righteousness by faith leads to keeping God's commandments. As we have seen, this happens not by man's efforts but by faith in Christ to manifest His commandment keeping in our lives.

Ellen White understood this when she wrote:

> The Lord in His great mercy sent a most precious message to His people through Elders Waggoner and Jones. This message was to bring more prominently before the world the uplifted Saviour, the sacrifice for the sins of the whole world. It presented justification through faith in the Surety; it invited the people to receive the righteousness of Christ, *which is made manifest in obedience to all the commandments of God.* (*Testimony to Ministers and Gospel Workers*, 91-92, emphasis added)

She knew that reception of the message of righteousness by faith would lead to "*obedience to all the commandments of God.*" Therefore, the message of righteousness by faith in Christ and the third angel's message are proclaimed to achieve the same goal—obedience to God's commandments.

Ellen White continued:

This is the message that God commanded to be given to the world. It is the third angel's message, which is to be proclaimed with a loud voice, and attended with the outpouring of His Spirit in a large measure. (Ibid.)

A Message That Prepares Believers and Glorifies Christ

It should be clear then that the message of righteousness by faith must be proclaimed to the world as we present the third angel's message. This is necessary for the full gospel of a delivering Savior to be proclaimed and prepare a people for Christ's second coming. For it is only as individuals understand and experience righteousness by faith in Christ alone that they will be able to live without a mediator when judgment ceases, remain faithful to God through the time of trouble, and stand in the presence of Christ in all His glory at His return and not be consumed.

It is only as righteousness by faith is understood and experienced that Jude's words will be true for us.

Now unto him that is able to keep you from falling, and to present you faultless before the presence of his glory with exceeding joy, To the only wise God our Saviour, be glory and majesty, dominion and power, both now and for ever. Amen. (Jude 24-25)

Therefore, since the Seventh-day Adventist Church was raised up by God to give the last-warning message to the world in preparation for Christ's second coming, it is essential the message of righteousness by faith be an integral part of our teaching and preaching. Our proclaiming only the warning of Revelation 14:9-11 will present prophetic facts of coming events. However, that alone will not give the hearers what they need in order to be ready for those final events.

The message of righteousness by faith must also be proclaimed so they will learn how to let Christ live out His commandment-keeping in and through them. Otherwise their obedience will actually become legalism, seeking to keep God's commandments through their own efforts, which is a meritorious obedience. When righteousness by faith is understood and experienced, Christ is actually doing the obedience in the life. Therefore, Christ alone gets the glory.

That no flesh should glory in his presence. But of him are ye in Christ Jesus, who of God is made unto us wisdom, and righteousness, and sanctification, and redemption: That, according as it is written, He that glorieth, let him glory in the Lord. (1 Corinthians 1:29-31)

Chapter Nine

The 1888 Message and the Last Generation

S eventh-day Adventists have always had what might be called a "last-generation theology." This theology teaches that the last generation of Christians that are living when Jesus comes will need to have developed a relationship with Christ as no other generation before them. This will be necessary because they will have to be faithful to God through the time of trouble (Revelation 13:12, 15), live in the presence of God without a mediator (Daniel 12:1), and stand in the presence of Christ in all His glory at His return (Jude 24) and not be consumed while all other inhabitants of earth will be destroyed by the brightness of His coming (2 Thessalonians 2:8).

It is only those who understand and experience the 1888 message of righteousness by faith that will be able to endure these final events successfully.

Jones and Waggoner's Understanding

Jones and Waggoner understood this. In the following statement A. T. Jones quoted Revelation 10:7, which states that when the seventh angel begins to sound, the "mystery of God" will be finished. Then he wrote:

> But what is the mystery of God? "Christ in you, the hope of glory. God … manifest in the flesh." Then in these days that mystery is to be finished in one hundred and forth-four thousand people. God's work in human flesh. God being manifested in human flesh, in you and me, is to be finished. His work upon you and me is to be finished. We are to be perfected in Jesus Christ. By the Spirit we are to come unto a perfect man, unto the measure of the stature of the fullness of Christ. (*Lessons on Faith*, 150)

The Necessity of the Baptism of the Holy Spirit

As we have seen, the work of the Holy Spirit is essential in Christ manifesting Himself in His people. Christ lives in His children through the baptism of the Holy Spirit. Therefore, it is absolutely necessary for the last generation of believers to understand and experience the baptism of the Holy Spirit. Of this, Ellen White wrote:

> Nothing but the baptism of the Holy Spirit can bring up the church to its right position, and prepare the people of God for the fast approaching conflict. (*Manuscript Releases*, Vol. 2, 30)

She was very clear that receiving the baptism of the Holy Spirit is our only hope of being faithful to God during earth's final conflict.

The Dangerous Condition of the Church

According to the book of Revelation, the church is in a dangerous condition today (Revelation 3:14-21). She is described by God as being "lukewarm." If her condition doesn't change, she will be rejected by God, "spewed" out of his mouth. Therefore, before Jesus returns, the church must go through a major spiritual transformation. She must experience genuine revival and reformation. Ellen White understood this great need when she wrote:

> A revival of true godliness among us is our greatest and most urgent of all our needs. To seek this should be our first work. (*Selected Messages,* Book 1, 121)

Two things are necessary for revival to take place. They are prayer and the baptism of the Holy Spirit in the lives of God's people. Ellen White indicated in the following statements:

> A revival need be expected only in answer to prayer. (Ibid.)

> The baptism of the Holy Ghost as on the day of Pentecost will lead to a revival of true religion and the performance of many wonderful works. (*Selected Messages,* Book 2, 57)

As God's people personally experience the daily baptism of the Holy Spirit, Jesus will be living in them. He will begin to manifest Himself in their lives. It is essential they understand and experience righteousness by faith in order to understand how to let Jesus live out His life of victory over every temptation and sin in their lives. For this last generation must be living a life of complete victory over all temptation and sin. Although this is impossible in their own strength, as they learn how to let Christ live out His victory in them, they will have their own experience of victory.

A Time of Purification

Before the final events, a purifying work will take place in the hearts and lives of God's children who respond to God's call to be part of that last generation. In commenting on the prophet Malachi's reference to this time of purification (Malachi 3:1-4), Ellen White wrote:

> Says the prophet: "Who may abide the day of his coming? and who shall stand when he appeareth? for he is like a refiner's fire, and like

fullers' soap; and he shall sit as a refiner and purifier of silver; and he shall purify the sons of Levi, and purge them as gold and silver, that they may offer unto the Lord an offering in righteousness." Malachi 3:2, 3. Those who are living upon the earth when the intercession of Christ shall cease in the sanctuary above, are to stand in the sight of a holy God without a mediator. Their robes must be spotless, their characters must be purified from sin by the blood of sprinkling. Through the grace of God and their own diligent effort, they must be conquerors in the battle with evil. While the investigative Judgment is going forward in Heaven, while the sins of penitent believers are being removed from the sanctuary, there is to be a special work of purification, of putting away of sin, among God's people upon earth. This work is more clearly presented in the messages of Revelation 14.

When this work shall have been accomplished, the followers of Christ will be ready for his appearing. "Then shall the offering of Judah and Jerusalem be pleasant unto the Lord, as in the days of old, and as in former years." Malachi 3:4. Then the church which our Lord at his coming is to receive to himself will be "a glorious church, not having spot, or wrinkle, or any such thing." Ephesians 5:27. Then she will look forth "as the morning, fair as the moon, clear as the sun, and terrible as an army with banners." (*The Great Controversy*, 425)

Notice several very important points in this statement. The prophet Malachi foretold of a time just prior to Christ's second coming when a great refining process would take place among God's people. This purifying process will cause God's children to have spotless characters. They will have been conquerors over every temptation and sin in their lives. Ellen White wrote of this experience:

Christ is waiting with longing desire for the manifestation of Himself in His church. When the character of Christ shall be perfectly reproduced in His people, then He will come to claim them as His own. (*Christ's Object Lessons*, 69)

Note also, that Ellen White says the character of Christ will be "perfectly reproduced in His people." This is not justification only where Christ's righteousness is imputed to the sinner. She refers here to Christ's perfect character being imparted to His people. Christ will be fully and perfectly manifesting His character in and through them. This happens only as they experience righteousness by faith in Christ alone. Also, it is the only way they can live in the sight of a holy God without a mediator.

When Ellen White referred to this purification process happening "through the grace of God and their own diligent effort," she referenced to the diligent watchfulness they have practiced in order to allow Christ to shine out in their lives at every point of temptation. They have been putting forth diligent effort in studying God's Word so they can be very aware of God's will in their lives. They have also been diligent in keeping a moment-by-moment communion with their Lord and maintaining meaningful personal prayer time(s) with God every day.

These verses in Malachi are followed by God's warning of judgment.

> And I will come near to you to judgment; and I will be a swift witness against the sorcerers, and against the adulterers, and against false swearers, and against those that oppress the hireling in his wages, the widow, and the fatherless, and that turn aside the stranger from his right, and fear not me, saith the Lord of hosts. (Malachi 3:5)

This judgment of the living takes place just before Christ's work as our mediator ends and Jesus returns. We must have experienced the purification in verses one through four in order to be judged righteous. Since we can only be righteous in Christ, it is absolutely necessary for us to understand and experience righteousness by faith in Christ to the fullest in our lives; both justifying and sanctifying righteousness.

A Time Without Sin

Also, when Christ is no longer mediating as our high priest, we must have attained a condition of complete victory over all sin in our lives. We will not be living in any known sin. We will not be sinning in thought, word, or deed. Christ will be fully manifesting Himself in and through our lives. In relation to this Ellen White wrote:

> "The prince of this world cometh," said Jesus, "and hath nothing in Me." John 14:30. There was in Him nothing that responded to Satan's sophistry. He did not consent to sin. Not even by a thought did He yield to temptation. So it may be with us. (*Desire of Ages*, 123)

This must be the experience of those who are ready to meet Jesus since they will no longer have the mediatory intercession of Christ to turn to if they sin. That may sound like an impossibility; yet, it is true. The 1888 message of righteousness by faith was all about how to experience that level of obedience to God; through the power of the Spirit within and faith in Christ's righteousness.

> There is therefore now no condemnation to them which are in Christ Jesus, who walk not after the flesh, but after the Spirit. For the law of the Spirit of life in Christ Jesus hath made me free from the law of sin and death. For what the law could not do, in that it was weak through the flesh, God sending his own Son in the likeness of sinful flesh, and for sin, condemned sin in the flesh: That the righteousness of the law might be fulfilled in us, who walk not after the flesh, but after the Spirit. (Romans 8:1-4)

Get Ready for the Latter Rain

The victory over temptation and sin must happen in our lives under the early-rain baptism power of the Holy Spirit. If this does not happen, the latter rain of the Spirit will be of no benefit to us. Ellen White wrote:

> I saw that many were neglecting the preparation so needful, and were looking to the time of 'refreshing' and the 'latter rain' to fit them to stand in the day of the Lord, and to live in His sight. Oh, how many I saw in the time of trouble without a shelter! They had neglected the needful preparation; therefore they could not receive the refreshing that all must have to fit them to live in the sight of a holy God. (*Christian Experience and Teachings of Ellen White*, 112)

It is a deception of Satan if we think that we do not have to take seriously the sin problem in our lives. Ellen White confirmed this with the words:

> I saw that none could share the "refreshing" [latter rain] unless they obtained the victory over every besetment, over pride, selfishness, love of the world, and over every wrong word and action. (Ibid., 113)

The early or former rain of the Spirit, which is the baptism of the Holy Spirit, gives us the spiritual maturity required in order to benefit from the latter rain.

> The latter rain, ripening earth's harvest, represents the spiritual grace that prepares the church for the coming of the Son of man. But unless the former rain has fallen, there will be no life; the green blade will not spring up. Unless the early showers have done their

work, the latter rain can bring no seed to perfection. (*The Faith I Live By*, 333)

Full spiritual growth under the early-rain baptism of the Spirit is necessary for us to even be able to recognize the latter rain of the Spirit when it is falling.

Unless we are daily advancing in the exemplification of the active Christian virtues, we shall not recognize the manifestation of the Holy Spirit in the latter rain. It may be falling on hearts all around us, but we shall not discern or receive it. (*Testimony to Ministers and Gospel Workers*, 507)

Hence, we must understand and experience righteousness by faith in Christ alone in order to be ready for the latter rain of the Spirit.

God's Call Today
In this light, it is absolutely vital that every Christian take seriously God's call to be filled with His Spirit and allow Jesus to manifest Himself in and through them; to experience righteousness by faith. Only then will they gain the victory over every temptation and sin in their lives. This is why Ellen White wrote:

Nothing but the baptism of the Holy Spirit can bring up the church to its right position, and prepare the people of God for the fast approaching conflict. (*Manuscript Releases*, Vol. 2, 30)

The 1888 message of righteousness by faith is a message of the complete victory we can have over the temptations and sins in our lives. It is necessary for every Christian to understand and experience righteousness by faith if they are living when Jesus comes.

Plus, sin is a matter of the heart; not simply acts of disobedience. Only God can change the heart by His Spirit through the righteousness of Christ in us (Romans 5:5; Galatians 5:22-23).

However, if one does not understand the true message of righteousness by faith, he will fall into one of two false teachings.

- If he is strongly committed to obey all of God's requirements, he will enter into the counterfeit called "legalism." He will seek to become holy through his own efforts, asking for God's help and power to be added to his efforts. This kind of religious experience carries with it a heavy burden and is joyless because he knows not the joy of the deliverance Christ offers.

- Or he admits defeat in trying to obey all of God's requirements because he has discovered that it is impossible for him to obey to this degree. He will develop an attitude that obedience to all of God's requirements cannot be done. So he quits trying and lives a very nominal Christian life. He says in his heart, "God forgives my shortcomings and will finally deliver me from my besetting sins when Jesus comes." He will also be forced to reject the concept of living without Christ as mediator during the time of trouble.

Is it any wonder why Satan fought so hard in 1888, and the years that followed, to obscure the message of righteousness by faith? As a denomination, we have gone through the legalism, and many today have fallen into nominal Christian living.

Satan doesn't care onto which side of error we fall, just as long as we do not discover the truth about righteousness by faith in Christ alone. I pray the Lord will overrule Satan's efforts today to hinder the reception of this vital message and experience in Christ. May God open all our eyes to the truth of righteousness by faith in Christ alone (Ephesians 1:17-19).

Chapter Ten

Preachers of Righteousness in Past Generations

T hus far in this book, besides the Bible I have quoted Ellen White,
A. T. Jones, and E. J. Waggoner on the subject of righteousness by
faith. We have seen that the Lord sought to deliver this wonderful
truth to our denomination in 1888. However, this was not a "new" truth.
Rather, it was a "present" truth. Ellen White wrote of how many of those
who labored in our denomination did not understand the truth of righteousness by faith.

> A veil has seemed to be before the eyes of many who have labored
> in the cause, so that when they presented the law, they have not
> had views of Jesus, and have not proclaimed the fact that, where
> sin abounded, grace doth much more abound. It is at the cross
> of Calvary that mercy and truth meet together, where righteous-
> ness and peace kiss each other. The sinner must ever look toward
> Calvary; and with the simple faith of a little child, he must rest in
> the merits of Christ, accepting His righteousness and believing in
> His mercy. Laborers in the cause of truth should present the righ-
> teousness of Christ, not as new light but as precious light that has
> for a time been lost sight of by the people. We are to accept Christ
> as our personal Saviour, and He imputes unto us the righteousness
> of God in Christ. Let us repeat and make prominent the truth that
> John has portrayed: "Herein is love, not that we loved God, but
> that he loved us, and sent his Son to be the propitiation for our
> sins" (1 John 4:10). (*Selected Messages*, Book 1, 383-384)

Through the ages the Lord has had His faithful people. Even today,
many of God's sincere children can be found in the various Christian de-
nominations. Just before Christ returns, a call will be made for them to
"come out" (Revelation 18:4) and stand with God's remnant people in proclaiming the third angel's message.

When I first came to understand the biblical teaching on the sanctification aspect of righteousness by faith, I began wondering if other
Christians in the past understood it. I have not read a great number of
other Christian authors. However, I have read a few. In my reading, I have
discovered some who did understand to a great degree this message of
righteousness by faith. However, they didn't understand the third angel's
message, the Sabbath, or have the prophetic views we have. Still, they did

understand the gospel and shared the wonderful good news of righteousness through Christ alone.

There have been God's children in all generations in New Testament times that understood the truth of Christ living in His people through the Holy Spirit, and that victory is achieved only by letting Him live out His life in them. Paul wrote of this to the church in Colossae.

> The mystery which hath been hid from ages and from generations, but now is made manifest to his saints: To whom God would make known what is the riches of the glory of this mystery among the Gentiles; which is Christ in you, the hope of glory. (Colossians 1:26-27)

Righteousness by faith is the mystery of God that was hid through the ages, but as Paul wrote, "Now is made manifest to his saints." The mystery of righteousness by faith has been available for God's people to understand and experience throughout the New Testament era of the Christian church. Yet, only a few of God's people have come to truly understand and experience the fullness of this mystery, which is Christ in us manifesting His righteousness to obey all of God's commandments.

So in this chapter I quote a few faithful ones who did understand and experience this mystery and have written on the subject. My purpose in presenting these quotes is to give a better understanding of this marvelous truth.

Walter Marshall

Walter Marshall was a seventeenth-century Christian author. His style of writing is somewhat tedious as compared to modern-day English writing styles. Yet, what he presents on the subject in his book, *Gospel Mystery of Sanctification*, is enlightening. Therefore, I have chosen to include quotes from him on the sanctification aspect of righteousness by faith.

Page 21:

> One great mystery is, that the holy frame and disposition by which our souls are furnished and enabled for immediate practice of the law, must be obtained by receiving it out of Christ's fullness, as a thing already prepared and brought to an existence for us in Christ, and treasured up in Him; and that as we are justified by a righteousness wrought out in Christ, and imputed to us; so we are sanctified by such a holy frame and qualifications, as are first wrought out, and completed in Christ for us, and then imparted to us. And as our natural corruption was produced originally in

the first Adam, and propagated from him to us; so our new nature and holiness is first produced in Christ, and derived from Him to us, or as it were propagated. So that we are not at all to work together with Christ, in making or producing that holy frame in us, but only to take it to ourselves, and use it in our holy practice, as made ready to our hands. Thus we have fellowship with Christ, in receiving that holy frame of spirit that was originally in Him. ... This mystery is so great, that notwithstanding all the light of the gospel, we commonly think that we must get a holy frame by producing it anew in ourselves, and by forming and working it out of our own hearts. Therefore many that are seriously devout, take a great deal of pains to mortify their corrupt nature, and beget a holy frame of heart in themselves, by striving earnestly to master their sinful lusts, and by pressing vehemently on their hearts many motives to godliness, laboring importunately to squeeze good qualifications out of them, as oil out of a flint. They account, that though they be justified by a righteousness wrought out by Christ, yet they must be sanctified by a holiness, wrought out by themselves. And though, out of humility, they are willing to call it infused grace; yet they think they must get the infusion of it by the same manner of working, as if it were wholly acquired by their own endeavors. On this account they acknowledge the entrance into a godly life to be harsh and unpleasing, because it costs so much struggling with their own hearts and affections, to new frame them. If they knew that this way of entrance is not only harsh and unpleasant, but altogether impossible; and that the true way of mortifying sin, and quickening themselves to holiness, is by receiving a new nature, out of the fullness of Christ; and that we do no more to the production of a new nature, than of original sin, though we do more to the reception of it. If they knew this, they might save themselves many a bitter agony, and a great deal of misspent burdensome labor, and employ their endeavors to enter in at the straight gate, in which a way as would be more pleasant and successful.

Page 95-96:

Despair of purging the flesh, or natural man of its sinful lusts and incinerations, and of practicing holiness, by your willing and resolving to do the best that lies in your own power, and trusting on the grace of God and Christ, to help you in such resolutions and endeavors; rather resolve to trust on Christ, to work in you to will and do, by his own power, according to his own good pleasure.—They that are convinced of their own sin and misery, do commonly first think to tame the flesh, and to subdue and root out its lusts, and to make their corrupt nature to be better natured, and inclined to holiness, by their struggling and wrestling with it: And, if they can but bring their hearts to a full purpose and resolution to do the best that lies in them, they hope, that, by such a resolution, they shall be able to achieve great enterprises, in the conquest of their lusts, and the performance of the most difficult duties. ... they trust on low carnal things for holiness, and upon the acts of their own will, their purposes, resolutions, and endeavors, instead of Christ: and they thrust on Christ to help them in this carnal way: whereas true faith would teach them, that they are nothing, and that they do but labor in vain. ... They that would cure it, and make it holy, by their own resolutions and endeavors, do act quite contrary to the design of Christ's death; for, he died, not that the flesh, or old natural man, might be made holy; but that it might be crucified, and destroyed out of us (Romans 6:6); and that we might live but by Christ living in us, and by His "spirit bringing forth the fruits of righteousness in us" (Galatians 2:20; 5:24-25).

And it is likely the Pharisee would trust on God, to help him in duty, as he would thank God for the performance of duty (Luke 18:11). And this is all the faith that many make use of in order to a holy practice. ... We must also take heed of depending for holiness upon any resolution to walk in Christ, or any written covenants, or any holiness, that we have already received; for, we must know, that the virtue of these things continues no longer than we continue walking in Christ, and Christ in us. They must be kept up by the continual presence of Christ in us; as light is maintained by the presence of the sun, and cannot subsist without it.

Charles Finney

Charles Finney served the Lord as a very successful evangelist in the 1800s. Ellen White mentions him in her writings. He too understood true biblical sanctification through the righteousness of Christ. I quote the following excerpts from his book, *Power from God.*

Page 119-126:

In all my Christian life, I have been pained to find so many Christians living in the legal bondage described in the seventh chapter of Romans—a life of sinner, resolving to reform and falling again. And what is particularly saddening, and even agonizing, is that many ministers and leading Christians give completely false instruction on how to overcome sin. The directions that are generally given on this subject, I am sorry to say, amount to this: "Take your sins in detail, resolve to abstain from them, and fight against them, if need be with prayer and fasting, until you have overcome them. Set your will firmly against a relapse into sin, pray and struggle, and resolve that you will not fall—and persist in this until you form the habit of obedience and break all your sinful habits." To be sure, it is generally added. "In this conflict, you must not depend upon your own strength but pray for the help of God." In a word, much of the teaching, both of the pulpit and the Christian press really amounts to this: sanctification is by works, and not by faith.

This, it will be perceived, is directing the attention to the overt act of sin, its source or occasions. Resolving and fighting against it fastens the attention on the sin and its source, and diverts it entirely from Christ.

Now, what is resolved against this religion of resolutions and efforts to suppress sinful habits and form holy habits? "Love is the fulfilling of the law" (Romans 13:10). But do we produce love by resolution? Do we eradicate selfishness by resolution? No, indeed. We may suppress this or that expression or manifestation of selfishness by resolving not to do this or that and by praying and struggling against it. We may resolve upon an outward obedience and work ourselves up to the letter of an obedience to God's commandments. But to eradicate selfishness from the heart by resolution is an absurdity.

All our battling with sin in the outward life by the force of resolution only ends in making us whitened sepulchers. All our battling with desire by the force of resolution is of no avail.

The fact is that it is simply by faith that we receive the Spirit of Christ to work in us "to will and to do according to his good pleasure" (Philippians 2:13). He sheds abroad His own life in our hearts and thereby kindles ours. (See Romans 5:5)

Every victory over sin is by faith in Christ. Whenever the mind is diverted from Christ by resolving and fighting against sin, whether we are aware of it or not, we are acting in our own strength; we are rejecting the help of Christ and are under a specious delusion. Nothing but the life and energy of the Spirit of Christ within us can save us from sin, and trust is the uniform and universal condition of the working of this saving energy within us.

It is rooted so deeply that one of the hardest lessons for the human heart to learn is to renounce self-dependence and trust wholly in Christ. When we open the door by implicit trust, He enters in and takes up His abode with us and in us. By shedding abroad His love, he quickens our whole soul into harmony with Himself, and in this way—and in this way alone—he purifies our hearts through faith.

Oh, that it could be understood that the whole of the spiritual life that is in any man is received directly from the Spirit of Christ by faith, as the branch receives its life from the vine! (See John 15:4-5). Away with this religion of resolutions! It is a snare of death. Away with this effort to make the life holy while the heart does not have in it the love of God!

Reuben A. Torrey

A Christian evangelist and revivalist who lived at the turn of the twentieth century was Reuben A. Torrey. He evangelized much in the cities of America. I have seen positive references about him and his Christian work in a book published by our denomination. He also understood the biblical teaching on righteousness by faith. I quote the following from his book, *Power Filled Living.*

Page 161:

It would be going too far to say we still had a carnal nature, for a carnal nature is a nature governed by the flesh. We have the flesh but in the Spirit's power, and it is our privilege to get daily, hourly, constant victory over the flesh and over sin. But this victory is not in ourselves, nor in any strength of our own. Left to ourselves, deserted of the Spirit of God, we would be as helpless as ever. It is still true that in us, that is, in our flesh, "nothing good dwells" (Romans 7:18). The victory is all in the power of the indwelling Spirit, but the Spirit's power may be in such fullness that one is not even conscious of the presence of the flesh. It seems as if the flesh were dead and gone forever, but it is only kept in the place of death by the Holy Spirit's power. If for one moment we were to take our eyes off Jesus Christ, if we were to neglect the daily study of the Word and prayer, down we would go. We must live in the

Spirit and walk in the Spirit if we would have continuous victory. (See Galatians 5:16, 25.) This life of the Spirit within us must be maintained by the study of the Word and prayer.

Page 165-166:

> It is the work of the Holy Spirit to form the living Christ within us, dwelling deep down in the deepest depths of our beings ... But by the power of the Holy Spirit bestowed on us by the risen Christ, we have Christ in us. Herein lies the secret of a Christlike life.
>
> We hear a great deal in these days about doing what Jesus would do. Certainly, as Christians, we ought to live like Christ. "He who says he abides in Him ought himself also to walk just as He walked" (1 John 2:6). But any attempt on our part to imitate Christ in our own strength will only result in utter disappointment and despair. There is nothing more futile that we can possibly attempt than to imitate Christ in the power of our will. If we imagine that we succeed, it will simply be because we have a very incomplete knowledge of Christ. The more we study Him, and the more perfectly we understand His conduct, the more clearly we will see how far short we have come from imitating Him. But God does not demand of us the impossible; He does not demand of us that we imitate Christ in our own strength. He offers to us something infinitely better. He offers to form Christ in us by the power of the Holy Spirit. And when Christ is thus formed in us by the Holy Spirit's power, all we have to do is to let this indwelling Christ live out His own life in us, and then we will be like Christ without struggles and effort of our own.
>
> No, we are not holy. To the end of our lives, in and of ourselves, we are full of weaknesses and failures, but the Holy Spirit is able to form within us the Holy One of God, the indwelling Christ. He will live out His life through us in all the humblest relations of life as well as in those that are considered greater.

Andrew Murray

Andrew Murray is a well-known Christian author who lived in the late nineteenth and early twentieth centuries. Several of his writings present the biblical teaching on righteousness by faith, and the following quotes are from his book, *Abiding in Christ.*

Page 23-25:

Referring to those who find the Christian life discouraging he wrote: "Dear soul! How little they know that the abiding in Christ is just meant for the weak, and so beautifully suited for their feebleness. It is not the doing of some great thing, and does not demand that we first lead a very holy and devoted life. No, it is simply weakness entrusting itself to a Mighty One to be kept—the unfaithful one casting self on One who is altogether trustworthy and true. Abiding in Him is not a work that we have to do as the condition for enjoying His salvation, but a consenting to let Him do all for us, and in us, and through us. It is a work He does for us—the fruit and the power of His redeeming love. Our part is simply to yield, to trust, and to wait for what He has engaged to perform."

Of those who try to obey God by putting forth their effort he wrote, "… The idea they have of grace is this—that their conversion and pardon are God's work, but that now, in gratitude to God, it is their work to live as Christians, and follow Jesus. There is always the thought of a work that has to be done, and even though they pray for help, still the work is theirs. They fail continually, and become hopeless; and the despondency only increases the helplessness. No, wandering one; as it was Jesus who drew you when He spake 'Come,' so it is Jesus who keeps you when He says 'Abide.'"

And if the question be asked, "But surely there is something for us to do?" the answer is, "Our doing and working are but the fruit of Christ's work in us." It is when the soul becomes utterly passive, looking and resting on what Christ is to do, that its energies are stirred to their highest activity, that we work most effectually because we know that He works in us.

Page 66:

Look not upon a life of holiness as a strain and an effort, but as the natural outgrowth of the life of Christ within you. And let ever again a quiet, hopeful, gladsome faith hold itself assured that all you need for a holy life will most assuredly be given you out of the holiness of Jesus. Thus will you understand and prove what it is to abide in Christ our sanctification.

Watchman Nee

Watchman Nee was a Chinese Christian who lived during the first half of the twentieth century. He is well known in many Christian circles. When persecution of Christians arose in China, he was imprisoned for his faith. He too understood the biblical teaching on righteousness by faith, and I quote from his book, *Sit, Walk, Stand*.

Page 22-23:

An engineer living in a large city in the West left his homeland for the Far East. He was away for two or three years, and during his absence his wife was unfaithful to him and went off with one of his best friends. On his return home he found he had lost his wife, his two children and his best friend. At the close of a meeting which I was addressing, this grief-stricken man unburdened himself to me. "Day and night for two solid years my heart has been full of hatred," he said. "I am a Christian, and I know I ought to forgive my wife and my friend, but though I try and try to forgive them, I simply cannot. Every day I resolve to love them and every day I fail. What can I do about it?" "Do nothing at all," I replied. "What do you mean?" he asked, startled. "Am I to continue to hate them?" So I explained: "The solution of your problem lies here, that when the Lord Jesus died on the Cross he not only bore your sins away but he bore you away too. When he was crucified, your old man was crucified in him, so that that unforgiving you, who simply cannot love those who have wronged you, has been taken right out of the way in his death. God has dealt with the whole situation in the Cross, and there is nothing left for you to deal with. Just say to him, "Lord, I cannot love and I give up trying, but I count on thy perfect love. I cannot forgive, but I trust thee to forgive instead of me, and to do so henceforth in me."

The man sat there amazed and said, "That's all so new. I feel I must do something about it." Then a moment later he added again, "But what can I do?" "God is waiting till you cease to do," I said. "When you cease doing, then God will begin … God is waiting for your store of strength to be utterly exhausted before he can deliver you. Once you have ceased to struggle, he will do everything. God is waiting for you to despair."

Page 34-41:

Our conduct and behavior depend fundamentally upon our inward rest in Christ.

He (Paul) has come to a place of rest in God. As a result his walking is not based on his efforts but on God's mightily inward working. There lies the secret of his strength. Paul has seen himself seated in Christ; therefore his walking before men takes its character from Christ dwelling in him.

Often we try to be meek and gentle without knowing what it means to let God work in us the meekness and gentleness of Christ. We try to show love, and finding we have none, we ask the Lord for love. Then we are surprised that he does not seem to give it to us.

You were surely not wrong in seeking love from God? No, but you were wrong in seeking that love as something in itself, a kind of package commodity, when what God desires is to express through you the love of his Son.

God has given us Christ. There is nothing now for us to receive outside of him. The Holy Spirit has been sent to produce what is of Christ in us; not to produce anything that is apart from or outside of him.

Recall once again the great words of 1 Corinthians 1:30. Not only did God set us, "in Christ." By him also "Christ Jesus ... was made unto us wisdom from God, and righteousness and sanctification, and redemption." This is one of the grandest statements in Scripture. He "was made unto us ..." If we believe this, we can put in there anything we need, and can know that God has made it good, for, through the Holy Spirit within us, the Lord Jesus is himself made unto us whatever we lack. We have been accustomed to look upon holiness as a virtue, upon humility as a grace, upon love as a gift to be sought from God. But the Christ of God is himself everything that we shall ever need.

Many a time in my need I used to think of Christ as a Person apart, and failed to identify him in this practical way with the "things" I felt so strongly the lack of. For two whole years I was groping in that kind of darkness, seeking to amass the virtues that I felt sure should make up the Christian life, and getting nowhere in the effort. And then one day—it was in the year 1933—light broke from heaven for me, and I saw Christ ordained of God to be made over to me in his fullness. What a difference! Oh the emptiness of "things" held by us out of relation to Christ that are dead. Once we see this it will be the beginning of a new life for us. Our holiness will be spelled thereafter with a capital H, our love with a capital L. He himself is revealed as the answer in us to all God's demands.

Go back now to that difficult brother, but this time, before you go, address God thus: "Lord, it is clear to me at last that in myself I cannot love him at all; but I know now that there is a life with me, the life of thy Son, and that the law of that life is to love. It cannot but love him." There is no need to exert yourself. Repose in him. Count upon his life. Dare thus to go and see that brother and to speak to him—and here is the amazing thing! Quite unconsciously (and I would emphasize the word "unconsciously," for the consciousness only comes afterwards) you find yourself speaking most pleasantly to him; quite unconsciously you love him; quite unconsciously you know him as your bother. You converse with him freely and in true fellowship, and on your return you find yourself saying with amazement; "Why, I did not exercise the least bit of anxious care just now, and yet I did not become in the least bit irritable? In some unaccountable way the Lord was with me and his love triumphed."

The operation of his life in us is in a true sense spontaneous, that is to say, it is without effort of ours. The all-important rule is not to "try" but to "trust," not to depend upon our own strength but upon his.

Too many of us are caught acting as Christians. The life of many Christians today is largely a pretense. They live a "spiritual" life, talk a "spiritual" language, adopt "spiritual" attitudes, but they are doing the whole thing themselves. It is the effort involved that should reveal to them that something is wrong. They force themselves to refrain from doing this, from saying that, from eating the other, and how hard they find it all!

Our life is the life of Christ, mediated in us by the indwelling Holy Spirit himself, and the law of that life is spontaneous. The moment we see that fact we shall end our struggling and cast away our pretense. Nothing is so hurtful to the life of a Christian as acting; nothing so blessed as when our outward efforts cease and our attitudes become natural—when our words, our prayers, our very life, all become a spontaneous and unforced expression of the life within.

God does not command what he will not perform; but we must throw ourselves back on him for this performance.

Has God commanded something? Then throw yourself back on God for the means to do what he has commanded.

Oswald Chambers

Oswald Chambers was a well-known, twentieth-century Christian author who died while still a young man. Yet, his short life has impacted many for Christ. One of his best known works is the daily devotional, *My Utmost for His Highest.* I quote from the July 23 reading entitled, "Sanctification."

But of Him you are in Christ Jesus, who became for us … sanctification. (1 Corinthians 1:30)

The Life Side: The mystery of sanctification is that the perfect qualities of Jesus Christ are imparted as a gift to me, not gradually, but instantly once I enter by faith into the realization that He "became for [me] … sanctification." Sanctification means nothing less than the holiness of Jesus becoming mine and being exhibited in my life.

The most wonderful secret of living a holy life does not lie in imitating Jesus, but in letting the perfect qualities of Jesus exhibit themselves in my human flesh. Sanctification is "Christ in you." (Colossians 1:27). It is His wonderful life that is imparted to me in God's grace. Am I willing for God to make sanctification as real in me as it is in His Word?

Sanctification means the impartation of the holy qualities of Jesus Christ to me. It is the gift of His patience, love, holiness, faith, purity, and godliness that is exhibited in and through every sanctified soul. Sanctification is not drawing from Jesus the power to be holy—it is drawing from Jesus the very holiness that was exhibited in Him, and that he now exhibits in me. Sanctification is an impartation, not an imitation. Imitation is something altogether different. The perfection of everything is in Jesus Christ, and the mystery of sanctification is that all the perfect qualities of Jesus are at my disposal. Consequently, I slowly but surely begin to live a life of inexpressible order, soundness, and holiness—"… kept by the power of God." (1 Peter 1:5)

Ellen White

Ellen White, of course, is well known by every Seventh-day Adventist. I have chosen two quotes from her writings to include in this chapter. These two quotes clearly specify that our obedience is the result of Christ manifesting Himself in our lives.

> All true obedience comes from the heart. It was heart work with Christ. And if we consent, He will so identify Himself with our thoughts and aims, so blend our hearts and minds into conformity to His will, that when obeying Him we shall be but carrying out our own impulses. The will, refined and sanctified, will find its highest delight in doing His service. When we know God, as it is our privilege to know Him, our lives will be a life of continual obedience. Through an appreciation of the character of Christ, through communion with God, sin will become hateful to us. (*Desire of Ages*, 668)

> When His words of instruction have been received, and have taken possession of us, Jesus is to us an abiding presence, controlling our thoughts, and ideas and actions ... It is no more we that live, but Christ that liveth in us, and he is the hope of glory. Self is dead, but Christ is a living Saviour. (*Testimonies to Ministers and Gospel Workers*, 389)

Conclusion

I don't endorse everything these non-Adventist authors teach. However, I have discovered that our loving, merciful God has not left his "other sheep" without teachers to lead them into a closer relationship with Christ. It is important that God's children outside the Adventist church grow in their experience of righteousness by faith in Christ alone because during the loud cry under the latter rain of the Spirit, people throughout Christendom will respond to the third angel's message and take their stand with God's remnant people (Revelation 18:4).

As we have seen in another chapter, those ready to meet Jesus when He returns will understand and experience righteousness by faith to the fullest. This is the only way they can stand in the presence of Christ in all His glory and not be consumed. Jesus described this wonderful event with the words:

> And then shall appear the sign of the Son of man in heaven: and then shall all the tribes of the earth mourn, and they shall see the Son of man coming in the clouds of heaven with power and great

glory. And he shall send his angels with a great sound of a trumpet, and they shall gather together his elect from the four winds, from one end of heaven to the other. (Matthew 24:30-31)

God's people inside and outside the Adventist church will have had to grow into the fullness of Christ during the preparation time just prior to His coming. The significance of Seventh-day Adventists receiving the message of righteousness by faith is that this experience will prepare the way for God to give the loud cry of the third angel's message through them. Furthermore, God has called the Seventh-day Adventist Church to give the loud cry under the power of the latter rain of the Spirit when the latter rain is poured out. It is during this loud cry that multitudes will "come out" and become part of God's remnant people.

The sad truth for Adventists is that those who reject the message of righteousness by faith bestowed by a merciful God will be shaken from among God's people. As Ellen White stated they will not recognize it as the work of the Holy Spirit.

> There is to be in the [Seventh-day Adventist] churches a wonderful manifestation of the power of God, but it will not move upon those who have not humbled themselves before the Lord, and opened the door of the heart by confession and repentance. In the manifestation of that power which lightens the earth with the glory of God, they will see only something which in their blindness they think dangerous, something which will arouse their fears, and they will brace themselves to resist it. Because the Lord does not work according to their ideas and expectations, they will oppose the work. "Why," they say, "should not we know the Spirit of God, when we have been in the work so many years?"—Because they did not respond to the warnings, the entreaties of the messages of God, but persistently said, "I am rich, and increased with goods, and have need of nothing." (*Review and Herald*, December 23, 1890)

In another statement, she wrote that those who reject the message of righteousness by faith in Christ alone will call this message "false light" even though it comes directly from God.

> The third angel's message will not be comprehended, the light which will lighten the earth with its glory will be called a false light, by those who refuse to walk in its advancing glory. (*Review and Herald*, May 27, 1890)

In 1888, some questioned if the message of righteousness by faith was the third angel's message. To this question, Ellen White wrote:

> Several have written to me, inquiring if the message of justification by faith is the third angel's message, and I have answered, "It is the third angel's message in verity." (*Review and Herald*, April 1, 1890)

Hence, it is by God's people understanding and experiencing the message of righteousness by faith, and sharing their experience that the earth is lightened with God's glory or character (Revelation 18:1). It is this experience that enables Christ to manifest Himself fully in His people, which happens during the darkest time of earth's history just before Christ returns.

Chapter Eleven

Three Amazing Experiences

E very Christian's experience has both similarities and differences in their various walks with the Lord. Moreover, I do believe that the three experiences in Christ that have affected me most profoundly would do the same for every Christian.

The Born-again Experience

The first amazing experience every Christian has is the new birth under the power of the Holy Spirit. John referred to this born-again experience in his gospel.

> But as many as received him, to them gave he power to become the sons of God, even to them that believe on his name: Which were born, not of blood, nor of the will of the flesh, nor of the will of man, but of God. (John 1:12-13)

> Jesus answered and said unto him, Verily, verily, I say unto thee, Except a man be born again, he cannot see the kingdom of God. (John 3:3)

> That which is born of the flesh is flesh; and that which is born of the Spirit is spirit. (John 3:6)

The born-again experience came to me when I was in college. Its influence was so profound in my life that it totally changed my philosophy of life. I was raised in a good home, but secular. Religion played no significant role. So my values were those of the world. I took engineering to make money. My goal was worldly success.

After experiencing the born-again encounter with Christ through the Spirit, worldly values lost importance. In time, I left the profession of engineering to study for the ministry. Since that experience, the majority of my adult life has been full-time ministry for the Lord.

The Baptism of the Holy Spirit

The second amazing experience God wants every Christian to have is to receive the baptism of the Holy Spirit. Being born again is one thing, but being baptized by the Holy Spirit is quite another.

The disciples were converted to Jesus but powerless before the day of Pentecost. So Jesus commanded them to wait in prayer until they received the baptism of the Holy Spirit, which took place at the conclusion of a ten-day prayer meeting (Acts 1:4-5, 8; Acts 2:1-4).

The experience of being baptized by the Spirit gave great power to the disciples' teaching and preaching. Three thousand accepted Jesus and were baptized in water following Peter's sermon on the day of Pentecost.

In 1999, the Lord led me to study the subject of the baptism of the Holy Spirit. I discovered that I did not understand this important biblical teaching. As a result of my study I was convicted to have specific prayer to be filled with the Spirit.

My experience of receiving the baptism of the Holy Spirit did not involve feeling or any dramatic evidence at the time of the prayer. However, the next day I began seeing significant changes in my personal life. I began experiencing personal revival. I also began seeing more of the power of the Spirit in my ministry.

As God continued to open my understanding on the subject I was led to write several books on the baptism of the Holy Spirit and the experiences the Spirit wants to lead the Spirit-filled Christian into. After investing our savings in the printing of my first book, the Lord strongly impressed me that I was not to advertise the book. So, in order to have peace within myself, I simply gave the book to the Lord and said, "I have done what you have asked me to do. If not one copy of the book sells, that is OK."

Just at that time I was invited to appear on 3ABN and share some things on the baptism of the Holy Spirit. As the program began, Danny Shelton held up my first book, *The Baptism of the Holy Spirit*, and commented about it. God used that program to take the message in that book literally around the world. This has been done without any advertising or promoting by me.

Also, the Lord opened opportunities to share the teaching on the Holy Spirit I was learning from God's Word. However, He once again made it clear that I was never to try to initiate an appointment to speak on the Holy Spirit. To date, the Lord has led me to share this message nationally and internationally.

So the baptism of the Holy Spirit experience has proved to be the second most important and amazing experience in my Christian life.

Righteousness by Faith

Through the years as a Christian, I knew that I was missing something in my personal walk with the Lord. The Christian life was many times a burden. Victories over temptation were sporadic at best. The yoke of Christ didn't seem very light to me.

However, I would read various Christian authors and sensed there was more to the gospel of Jesus Christ. I knew the theory, but didn't see or experience the power for consistent victory. I would put forth effort to obey asking God to add His strength to my efforts. Yet, consistent victory seemed out of my grasp.

Then, as I was reading one day, I began to see more clearly the biblical teaching of how we are to let Jesus live out His life of victory over sin in our lives. I prayed earnestly for the Lord to open my understanding to this wonderful truth. I strained my mind to grasp it.

Then the light began to shine into my soul. Oh, what joy it brought. I finally began to see the glorious truth of true righteousness by faith in Christ alone for victory over temptation and sin. I began seeing that Christ is not only a sin-forgiving Savior, but a sin-delivering Savior.

I began applying what I was learning to areas of my life and found this wonderful teaching to be real and not just theory. I had finally discovered the truth of righteousness by faith in Christ. This experience revolutionized my walk with the Lord.

So the third most amazing experience in my Christian experience has been the discovery of the sanctification aspect of righteousness by faith. That led to the writing of my seventh book, *Spirit Baptism & Abiding in Christ.*

The 1888 Connection

As I have shared previously, through fellow believers, the Lord brought to my attention that what He had revealed to me was indeed similar to the 1888 message of righteousness by faith presented by Jones and Waggoner. I spent some time reflecting on the possibility of this connection. I began reading what Jones and Waggoner had written. I studied what Ellen White had said about the 1888 message. Then I began feeling convicted to write about the marvelous message of righteousness by faith that God gave to our denomination more than 100 years ago.

My prayer is that you will also experience the three amazing experiences that God offers each of us: the new birth, the baptism of the Holy Spirit, and experiencing righteousness by faith in Christ alone. When you enter into all three of these experiences, your joy in the Lord will be full. Jesus will become more precious to you than He has ever been. Your heart will be filled with praises to Him for what He has done and is doing for you, in you, and through you.

These three experiences will prepare you for the most amazing experience of all—the second coming of Christ in glory.

How true are the words of the song *Amazing Grace*:

"Amazing grace! How sweet the sound,
That saved a wretch like me!
I once was lost, but now am found,
Was blind, but now I see.

"Twas grace that taught my heart to fear,
And Grace my fears relieved;
How precious did that Grace appear
The hour I first believed!

"Through many dangers, toils, and snares,
I have already come;
Tis grace hath brought me safe thus far,
And grace will lead me home.

"When we've been there ten thousand years,
Bright shining as the sun,
We've no less days to sing God's praise
Than when we'd first begun."

Amazing Grace, by John Newton, taken from the *Seventh-day Adventist Hymnal*, hymn 108.

Yes, the born-again experience, the baptism of the Holy Spirit, and righteousness by faith in Christ are all amazing acts of God's grace.

Chapter Twelve

A Serious Warning

The following quotes from Ellen White are taken from the book, *Testimonies to Ministers and Gospel Workers* (pages are in parenthesis). She made some very serious statements about the 1888 message of righteousness by faith presented by Jones and Waggoner, and she gave some very serious warnings to those who rejected it. I believe these statements and warnings are very applicable today in the light that God is once again seeking to bring this wonderful truth to His people in preparation for Christ's second coming.

The Lord in His great mercy sent a most precious message to His people through Elders Waggoner and Jones. This message was to bring more prominently before the world the uplifted Saviour, the sacrifice for the sins of the whole world. It presented justification through faith in the Surety; it invited the people to receive the righteousness of Christ, which is made manifest in obedience to all the commandments of God. Many had lost sight of Jesus. They needed to have their eyes directed to His divine person, His merits, and His changeless love for the human family. … This is the message that God commanded be given to the world. It is the third angel's message, which is to be proclaimed with a loud voice, and attended with the outpouring of His Spirit in a large measure. …

The message of the gospel of His grace was to be given to the church in clear and distinct lines, that the world should no longer say that Seventh-day Adventists talk the law, the law, but do not teach or believe Christ. (91-92)

This is the testimony that must go throughout the length and breadth of the world. It presents the law and the gospel, binding up the two in a perfect whole. (94)

I would speak in warning to those who have stood for years resisting light and cherishing the spirit of opposition. How long will you hate and despise the messengers of God's righteousness? God has given them His message. They bear the word of the Lord. There is salvation for you, but only through the merits of Jesus Christ. The grace of the Holy Spirit has been offered you again and again. Light and power from on high have been shed abundantly in the midst of you …

Neglect this great salvation, kept before you for years, despise this glorious offer of justification through the blood of Christ and sanctification through the cleansing power of the Holy Spirit, and there remaineth no more sacrifice for sins, but a certain fearful looking for of judgment and fiery indignation. (97)

The Mystery of God Finished

Just before Jesus returns, the mystery of God will be finished.

But in the days of the voice of the seventh angel, when he shall begin to sound, the mystery of God should be finished, as he hath declared to his servants the prophets. (Revelation 10:7)

What is this mystery of God that is to be finished? Paul tells us.

The mystery which hath been hid from ages and from generations, but now is made manifest to his saints: To whom God would make known what is the riches of the glory of this mystery among the Gentiles; which is *Christ in you*, the hope of glory. (Colossians 1:26-27; emphasis added)

The 1888 message is all about the mystery of God—Christ in you, which is your only hope of glory. The mystery of God is the gospel of a sin-pardoning and sin-delivering Savior. The mystery of God is full justification and sanctification through Jesus Christ. The mystery of God is righteousness by faith in Christ alone.

This is the mystery that will be completed in God's people at the very end of time. That is why God is bringing this message again to His people at this hour of earth's history.

We place ourselves in grave jeopardy if we reject God's merciful call to understand and experience righteousness by faith as so many did more that 100 years ago.

I personally believe that today there will be a remnant among God's professed people who will respond to God's call and experience the full and complete deliverance Christ offers. They will be the people who receive benefit from the latter rain of the Spirit. They will give the loud cry of the third angel's message in great power. They will victoriously make it through the time of trouble or tribulation by not receiving the mark of the beast. And, they will be the ones who will stand in the very presence of Christ in all His glory and not be consumed.

God is calling you to be among that people.

Now unto him that is able to keep you from falling, and to present you faultless before the presence of his glory with exceeding joy, To the only wise God our Saviour, be glory and majesty, dominion and power, both now and for ever. Amen. (Jude 24-25)

Books by Pastor Smith

The Baptism of the Holy Spirit
This book presents the biblical teaching on the baptism of the Holy Spirit, the benefits of receiving this gift in fullness, and why it is necessary for the Christian to receive it.

Spirit Baptism & Evangelism
The relationship between the baptism of the Holy Spirit and witnessing for Christ is presented along with Christ's method of evangelism.

Spirit Baptism & New Wineskin Fellowship
This book gives a biblical and historical study into how the early Christians "did church," and why it is important Christians continue to experience genuine fellowship.

Spirit Baptism & Deliverance
It is God's will to deliver His children from every influence and oppression of Satan in the Christian's life spiritually, emotionally, and physically. This book presents how deliverance can become a reality in the Christian's life.

Spirit Baptism & Prayer
Prayer is the most powerful force on earth. This book presents the many facets of prayer including fasting and how to pray in the Spirit.

Spirit Baptism & Christ's Glorious Return
This book presents the characteristics of those who are ready for Christ's return.

Spirit Baptism & Abiding in Christ
This book explains how the Christian is to obtain victory over every temptation and sin by allowing Christ to live out His life in and through him or her. When this is experienced one's life will never again be the same.

Spirit Baptism & Waiting on God
This book presents the biblical teaching about waiting on God for everything: prayer, guidance, service, Christ's character, and why God allows trials and difficulties to enter the Christian's life.

Spirit Baptism & the 1888 Message of Righteousness by Faith
In 1888 God brought the message of righteousness by faith to the Seventh-day Adventist Church. This book presents what that message was and why it is essential that we experience righteousness by faith in Christ alone today.

Pastor Smith's books can be ordered from:
Adventist Book Center • 800-435-0008

Dennis Smith
16 West St, Woodbridge, CT 06525
Phone: 203-389-4784
Email: smith06515@msn.com